Praise for
Financial Advisors"

"Sales book? Think again. This wonderful new perspective is engaging and behavior changing. This carefully and well-written book dispels the adage of current sales hype and gives practical and specific instructions to winning new relationships and gaining predictable results. We have taken the concepts outlined in Randy's book to drive millions of dollars in added business to our firm. I would recommend that any executive, interested in improving sales teams' results, read this book and apply its concepts."

– Christian Jeppesen, Chief of Advisory Practices, First Trust Portfolios L.P

"Schwantz has taken the mysticism away from the "selling" part of this business. He takes you step-by-step on the journey of how to craft and refine your value proposition for clients and prospects alike in this watershed book. By following Randy's system, advisors (regardless of tenure) will see their closing ratios and qualified referrals improve dramatically in their practices. Stop "selling" and start using this Buying Facilitation Process today."

– William (Drew) Watson, Senior Financial Advisor, Ameriprise Financial Services, Inc.

"These strategies and techniques will create a competitive advantage for your managers, consultants, agencies or advisors. I would recommend The Wedge training for your firm to separate your offering from the competition. In this competitive environment where banks, brokers, accounting, and legal institutions are attempting to attract the same client through offering wealth management services, organizations using a proven and systematic process will continue to take market share."

– Jake Tomes, Level Four Group, LLC

"Randy has provided the financial industry with a powerful tool not just to increase sales, but to help clients understand the benefits of working with a professional. His insight into understanding what the consumer needs in order to take action is clear and easily understood, but more importantly, a structure one can implement. This is a must read for anyone in the financial services industry."

"Randy Schwantz clearly articulates a proven strategy that will help advisors more effectively gather assets in a competitive marketplace. The Million Dollar Advisor is a must read for anyone working with the affluent."

"Randy Schwantz has been using his process with great success for many, many years, and in his new book he explores how his techniques can help all types of financial advisors accelerate their practices. Randy is a great instructor, an innovative thinker, and a master at providing relevant solutions that will help sales people take their business to an entirely new level."

"Randy's methodologies are brilliant. Not only do we use his system to train our salespeople, we also use his techniques to secure our relationships with existing clients."

"If more financial advisors focused on winning clients instead of selling them, all clients and advisors would be better off. With his new book, Randy Schwantz shows them how to win!"

THE
WEDGE

FOR FINANCIAL ADVISORS

HOW TO STOP SELLING AND START WINNING

RANDY SCHWANTZ

This publication is designed to provide accurate and authoritative information in regard to the subject matter covered. It is sold with the understanding that the publisher is not engaged in rendering legal, accounting or other professional service. If legal advice or other expert assistance is required, the services of a competent professional should be sought. – **From a Declaration of Principles jointly adopted by a Committee of the American Bar Association and a Committee of Publishers and Associations.**

Circular 230 Notice – The content in this publication is not intended or written to be used, and it cannot be used, for the purposes of avoiding U.S. tax penalties.

ISBN: 978-0-87218-957-7

Library of Congress Control Number: 2007943361

1st Edition

Copyright © 2007
The National Underwriter Company
P.O. Box 14367, Cincinnati, Ohio 45250-0367

Printed in U. S. A.

Dedication

When the surgeon showed me the nickel-sized battery he'd pulled out of Payton's throat that had been lodged in there for 3 months, I was both relieved and angry. He said we were very lucky!

Here's what happened to my youngest daughter: It was late November, not that long until Christmas. Payton was 10 months old, crawling around, picking up everything in her sight, examining it, and moving on to the next thing. Everything was good; she was a beautiful child, healthy and on the move. With three older sisters there was a lot of anticipation for Christmas. Mom was secretly buying toys, putting batteries in them, and wrapping and storing them away out of sight. It was a busy time.

Payton was a great sleeper, particularly now that she had started to transition to oatmeal and the other cereals babies start eating after growing beyond momma's milk. She slept in her crib in our room. One night, in early December, I remember waking up to her loud breathing. Imagine the sound of someone out of breath, breathing hard to fill their lungs. I woke up my wife, Lori and asked her what she thought was going on with Payton. We got up, held her for a while and then put her back down; temporarily things were better, but not right.

Lori took Payton to the doctor the next day. He examined her and said it was allergies. "Wow" is all we could say. Anything you can do for her? "Not really," said the doctor, "She's too young." So for the next few weeks, every night we would hear that loud, uncomfortable breathing. I told Lori, "We've got to do something. This won't work." So we went to a new doctor to get a second opinion. Doctor #2 confirmed Doctor #1's assessment, "It must be allergies, and she's too young to treat. She'll grow out of it."

We immediately asked for a referral to an allergy expert, but with the state of PPOs and HMOs, that took about 6 weeks. In the meantime, Payton was starting to regurgitate everything she ate that had any texture to it at all. At mealtimes she was in her high chair, eating like a "pig" stuffing down corn and peas; and then she would first turn pale, then bright red, and then everything would come back up again. This happened time and time again while we were waiting to see the allergist. It was horrible, but there wasn't anything we could do about it. We both had that hopeless feeling every time it happened.

Finally, the appointment with the allergist rolled around and Lori accompanied Payton. The Doctor examined her and the first thing he asked was, "Has she had an x-ray"? "Well, no" Lori responded. Two days later, we got an x-ray at Children's Hospital in Dallas. This time I went with Lori to help her with Payton, by then 13-14 months old, as those big x-ray machines are a little bit scary; actually, in reality they're very scary to such a little kid.

I remember, as I was trying to assist the x-ray technician in getting her to lay still for just a micro-second so he could take the x-ray, Payton was screaming, crying, and kicking. Eventually, I succeeded in getting her pinned down for just a second so that he was able to pull the trigger. He then immediately said, "You've got to come here". On the screen we could see a round object, about the size of a nickel, approximately an inch below her chin. The technician said, "She swallowed a coin. How long has that been in there?" When I told him it had been two to three months, the tech said, "Oh, my gosh, we've got to get the surgeon in here right away." A few minutes later the surgeon came in, introduced himself, looked at the x-ray, and said, "We've got to get that out now!"

We filled out the paperwork and signed the release forms, and within 90 minutes she was in the operating room. Fifteen minutes later, the surgeon came to see us with a little baggie containing a round flat battery in his hand. He said he had to tug really hard to get it out of there, that it was lodged about 1½" down in her esophagus. He didn't say it, but you could tell he felt she was lucky to still be with us.

Here's the point:

The first two doctors that examined Payton both said it was allergies, live with it, there is nothing that can be done. Well, they were both wrong. It wasn't allergies, and, yes, there was something that could be done about it.

The point is that we all have things in our lives that aren't working. Many times we diagnose what we think is the problem, and yet, it's not the real problem. There is a solution if we are willing to dig deep and find the real cause.

According to a friend of mine, Chris Jeppesen, the typical Financial Advisor, 5 years in the business, has 1,100 positions, 290 packaged products, and 400 accounts. Many of them are stuck in a sea of molasses and have an uncontrollable business model that is hard to manage and hard to grow. Even more questionable is this: are they really serving their clients effectively?

As a result, there is an enormous number of investors that are being poorly served and don't know it. They too have learned to accept the status quo and a fair amount of unpredictability. How many investors don't know why their money is invested in the stocks and mutual funds that it is in? How many investors don't have a precise benchmark to which they are comparing performance? How many investors don't have separate buckets for education, weddings, cars, and retirement? I suspect the list could go on.

This book is intended to assist and help two kinds of advisors. One is the advisor that has it all together, is proactive, serves his clients extraordinarily well, and, like the surgeon, wants to rescue investors from those that are not capable of serving them at a predictable and effective level. The second type of advisor is the one that might have too many positions, too many packaged products, and too many clients and wants to take the first steps out of the molasses and into the light. They want to serve their clients better while also having a better lifestyle themselves. It's you we strive to serve.

I dedicate this book to my daughter Payton for two reasons. First, she brings great joy to our family and we all love her very much. Secondly, her story is a brutal reminder not to always accept what we've been told by the authorities as "truth," i.e. Doctors #1 and #2. We can, through thought and actions, make our lives better.

About the Author

Randy Schwantz is a leader and innovator in the field of Sales Performance. He creates and delivers thought-provoking presentations that allow him to connect with every member of his audience. He brings a passion and belief to his work that immediately engages seminar participants. His presentations have been called inspiring, provoking, and even outrageous.

Randy has spent over 15,000 hours in Sales Training and one-on-one coaching sessions converting Sellers to Winners of New Business and inspiring them to reach their personal and professional goals. Randy believes selling is hard for two reasons: First, many advisors have a difficult time articulating what they do different or better than their competitors (lack of differentiation). Secondly, most buyers have lowered their expectations down to the service levels they are currently receiving and are fundamentally content. Randy's approach is "very" non-traditional, in that most sales training focuses on learning the basic skills of listening, probing, overcoming objections, and closing, but fails to address the biggest threat to closing: The Incumbent Advisor. Randy helps advisors get the incumbent advisor fired, without saying anything bad about them, by helping them grasp their competitive advantage, and then coaching them in how to use it as a Wedge to get the prospect to "discover their hidden pain" resulting from being underserved by their current advisor. Net result: more wins—faster!

On the personal side, Randy lives near Dallas, Texas with his five biggest supporters: his wife Lori, and his four daughters. When he is not acting as a sideline coach/cheerleader at one of his daughters' basketball games, he is seeking out an adrenaline rush himself. A bit of a daredevil, he has participated in—and lived to tell about—firewalking, skydiving, parasailing, and improv comedy.

For more information on Randy and The Wedge Group, please visit www.thewedge.net/FA. To find out how you can bring The Wedge sales training into your firm, please email us at trainer@thewedge.net or if you are interested in having Randy speak at your next event, please email us at speaker@thewedge.net. If you prefer, feel free to call The Wedge Group at (877) 999-9334 or (214) 446-3209.

Table of Contents

Preface

As Financial Advisors, we oftentimes have to deal with some hard realities. One is that the market is uncontrollable. Historically it goes up, but it has also taken plenty of dips along the way. Unfortunately, our clients don't always remember the big picture and it causes us all a mix of misery and frustration at times when we help clients manage their emotions during turbulent market conditions.

There is another hard reality that we have to deal with, particularly when your goal is to move up market and grow your revenue stream. Almost every affluent prospect you target is currently being served by someone else. Several of them are well served by quality Financial Advisors. However, there are plenty that need your help but don't know it. So challenge Number One is getting them to see you. Challenge Number Two is that there is someone already occupying the chair you want, and that's the Incumbent Advisor. Here's the reality, the incumbents have to lose for you to win.

Be careful not to pre-judge this book or this concept at this early stage. Its purpose is simple, and its process is elegant. In fact, if you were the prospect of someone using this process you'd probably say it mirrors the way "I want to buy."

I believe that what you'll learn in this book is the very opposite of slinging trash at your competition, of overselling your capability; and it's in direct conflict of almost anything you'll learn in the traditional sales class. And here's why.

First of all, The Wedge deals with the truth: most clients don't want to be sold; they want to buy. Secondly, most people feel the best ideas are the ones they generate. Third, a cold reality is three people exist in almost every sales interview: the new buyer, you, and the incumbent advisor. And, someone has to lose for you to win.

Here is how this system called The Wedge really helped me. As a coach and consultant in the financial services industry, I first help advisors discover that their life, practice, and future are much bigger than what they can actually see.

From there, once their mindset is dialed into turbo growth mode, we work on the strategies, tactics, and specific techniques that will drive the big results they couldn't see in the beginning of our working relationship. This is where The Wedge comes in.

Fundamentally, the advisors I work with believe they do a better job than many of their competitors. My challenge is pretty simple, how do I get my advisors' prospects to see that they are being underserved by the incumbent advisor without ever saying anything bad about them? Secondly, how do I get my advisors' prospects to see how good they really are without my advisors having to tell the potential new customers? The Wedge taught me how to do that in such an easy and well-designed way that our advisors continue to rapidly increase their GDC (gross revenue/book of business) through new client acquisition and gathering additional assets from existing clients.

If you're like me and you desire to grow your GDC rapidly, then you've got to target relationships with significant assets and move your practice more up market. To win these clients you have to stop selling and start winning—Randy will thoroughly explain to you the vast differences between these two concepts in this profit-driving book.

Day in and day out, advisors with a high level of growth in their GDC and Assets Under Management are generally the ones who most deserve it. They've made decisions to position their practice in a way that attracts the "right" kind of clients—Top Shelf Clients—for them. They know they can't be everything to everybody. They've built systems and an infrastructure to support their service "promises" to clients. They can articulate their competitive advantages to clients in a magnetic and compelling way. More importantly, they know how to constructively and effectively take business from competitors by letting the clients fire their existing advisors. If you desire to be one of these advisors, this book will offer you tremendous wisdom in developing a better life and practice.

Travis Ray Chaney
CEO, Dynamic Directions – D2, Inc.

Chapter 1

Stop Selling and Start Winning

"What you do that your competition doesn't is where your prospect is under-served. Knowing that is the key to Winning and Growing Up Market!"

This book is the result of literally thousands of hours I have spent working with professionals like you who were motivated, intelligent, productive…and frustrated. Frustrated because they were not achieving the high goals they had set for themselves.

What I have learned in the past fifteen years has helped many of them achieve their personal goals of doubling or tripling their income, of having more time to invest in their families and personal relationships, and of achieving the professional success that eluded them for so long.

They couldn't understand why they weren't successful more often, why some opportunities that seemed all but certain one day frequently disappeared the next. What were they doing wrong?

Nothing. And everything.

Their mistake, the most common mistake made by businesspeople in America today, is their belief in "selling." Selling is important, but it is not the goal. Winning by helping your clients win is the goal, but you can't help them win unless they're your clients! Until you stop selling and start winning, you will never have the financial or personal success you desire.

"But Randy," a client asked me once, "How can I stop selling? I'm in sales....
I'm a salesperson for cryin' out loud! What am I supposed to do?"

I'm not a motivational speaker or New Age guru. I'm not selling chicken
soup for the salesman or the seven habits of the happy closer. I don't believe
in magic formulas or psychic energy.

I'm a businessman and a sales coach. I believe in techniques, strategies, and
sales tactics that have been proven to work because they've been tested under
fire, in the conference rooms and business suites and at the kitchen tables of
America. No stunts, no tricks, no gimmicks—just results.

Because I have spent so many years looking at the sales industry from a
practical, bottom-line viewpoint, I've learned, in a very practical way, that the
obstacle most professionals must overcome to succeed is their dependency
on "selling."

What is Selling?

The simplest definition of selling I can give you is this: Every time you sit
down with a prospect without a specific, well-developed, and effective strategy for winning, you are just selling. Period.

"If people understood how good you really are, who wouldn't want it?!"

Selling is killing you out in the marketplace. It is wasting your time and
your prospects. Anyone who says selling is hard is wrong. Selling is easy;
winning is hard. Selling means making a good presentation. Winning means
walking out with a rollover or transfer of a client's portfolio.

Selling is about looking good, prospecting, networking, "cocktailing,"
color-copying, binding, packaging, and e-mailing. Winning is about putting
money in the bank for you and your family!

In other words, selling is believing in the process, while winning is focusing
on the results and crafting a specific, workable, well-rehearsed method to achieve
those results.

When you stop selling and start winning, you and your family, but equally important, your new clients, win!

Winning is when your client is significantly better off and so are you! (CBO & SRU)

What is Your Focus?

The difference between selling and winning is focus. When you're selling, you're focused on yourself. You know everything there is to know about your product, your service, your company. But you know almost nothing about the prospect you are calling on.

Because you're so focused on yourself, you can probably think of a hundred reasons why everyone ought to hire you and fire your competition, but you probably can't come up with one specific reason why it would benefit the prospect sitting right in front of you. Instead of a strategy to win by connecting with the prospect, your hope—"hope" is what you have left after you abandon hard work and planning—is that your products and services will somehow appeal to the prospect and that he or she will make the connection for you.

As a result, your success depends completely on others. Even if you have the best proposal, the best presentation, and the best personality, you are no closer to winning than the most amateur of your competitors. You're just counting on luck to get positive results for you.

What is Your Intent?

Another key difference is *intent*. The intent of the "seller" is merely to stay in the game, to have a shot at proposing or making an offer. Sellers are focused on opportunities to pitch and present.

The winner is looking for opportunities to win. He enters *every* prospect meeting with the intent to win. Winners aren't playing numbers games, they aren't throwing their ideas and proposals against a wall and hoping some will stick. They want every shot to count.

An example of this difference in intent would be two skiers at the top of a mountain. One skier is focused on just making it down the hill and nothing more. He just wants to make it back to the lodge in one piece so he can come out another day and do it again. Whether he makes good time or not doesn't matter. He just wants to make it down one more time.

The other skier is focused on the course. He's looking at the turns, the curves, the trees, and the obstacles. He's not thinking about himself, he's focused on the course and how it needs to be skied. He begins the course with a plan specific to this course that will let him make the best possible time.

Which skier is going to finish first? Which skier is going to be the most successful? The one whose focus is not on himself and whose intent is to master the problem at hand.

How To Tell If You're "Selling"

As a sales coach, I've worked with thousands of professionals, and I've noticed that many of them consider it a "win" just to get the chance to meet with a new prospect and propose a new opportunity. They interview, run plans, they crunch numbers, package it up, run it through the color printer, put it in a glossy binder and hand it to their prospect, and then take a victory lap.

This is the epitome of traditional selling: put a proposal in front of the prospect and either the prospect will hear something he likes, or he won't. The salesperson's job is simply to get in front of as many prospects as possible, propose, and try to close and wait for lightning to strike.

What's Wrong With "Selling?"

Selling wastes a lot of time on unqualified prospects. When you're selling, you're going through the motions: making calls, looking for a chance to prepare a proposal, playing the percentages. This makes advisors, in essence, peddlers. A peddler is a guy that knows his product pretty well and goes out telling everyone they should use it. It's a numbers game. "If I call on enough people, I'll make a sale." It's a low percentage game however; too much time is wasted in the process of preparing proposals for non-buyers. Time that could have been used to sharpen skills, investigate further the real needs of true prospects, and execute strategies to break incumbent relationships as your prospect wins and so do you!

Selling allows the prospect to "use" you. When you go into a meeting with a prospect who has no intention of buying, you aren't just wasting your time, you're wasting his or her time, too. How does the prospect benefit from this meeting? By using you as an educational resource. You spend an hour telling him about potential gaps in his financial plan; then, after you're gone, he calls the incumbent advisor to talk over those ideas and see if they should make a change to his current investment strategy.

> *The incumbent is the advisor who is currently providing your prospect investment products and services.*

Selling keeps the focus on you and your efforts, not on the real problem. To sellers, sales is like Olympic ice skating, a solo sport in which the performer wins or loses based solely on his or her performance. If you prepare yourself well, have the right attitude, hit all the marks, and dazzle the crowd, you will score enough points to skate away with a gold medal contract and a bouquet of lucrative clients.

But sales isn't a solo sport. Sales is a contact sport. It's not figure skating— it's ice hockey. Sales is a sport in which, more often than not, someone else— the incumbent—is on the ice, controlling the puck.

And until you take the puck out of the incumbent's control and put it back in play, there is no opportunity to succeed. You can have a presentation direct from Cecil B. de Mille, along with the positive attitude of Norman Vincent Peale, but as long as the incumbent is in control, the person you are meeting with is not a real prospect. He's just someone you are "selling" to.

The Two Problems Selling Can't Solve

The reason selling is so inefficient is that it is based on the faulty premise that there are two people in every prospect meeting (you and the prospect) and that the most important person in the process is you, the advisor. Nothing could be further from the truth.

There are, in fact, *three* people in every prospect meeting—you, the prospect, and the incumbent advisor—and you are the *least* important person in the group. The other two people will determine whether or not you win, and before you do, you must solve two key problems.

Problem Number 1: A Lack of Trust

The number one problem facing people in sales is building trust, enabling prospects to easily tell the truth. Overcome this problem, and you will become the most successful advisor in America.

Why do prospects hold back? Because they have no desire to be sold. Their job is to check out their options, so they want to meet with you and get educated without actually buying from you. However, most people find hurting the feelings of others by rejecting their offer to be an unpleasant experience, so they tell you "little white lies" instead.

How do they do that? By giving you part of what you want—the opportunity to compete and for them to review your offer. In your meetings they nod politely as you spew out the familiar sales pitch of "quality service, competitive fees, and commitment to satisfaction." They compliment you on your professional presentation and maybe even let you buy them lunch, but when it's over, they thank you and let you go off to your next meeting.

Most of the prospects you meet with have an interest in engaging in an honest dialogue with you, but how often do you make that difficult by "selling" instead of listening? What could be easier for a prospect than answering a couple of simple, open-ended "sales-school" questions they've heard a hundred times before, then drinking a cup of coffee while you babble on about abstract statistics and rehearsed sales pitches? In most sales presentations, if the prospect did want to have an honest dialogue about what he and his family wanted to accomplish, he would oftentimes have to interrupt the seller to do it!

Building trust, leading to an honest dialogue, involves effort and risk. If you don't stop "selling," your prospect might believe that you are no different from any other advisor. And since doing nothing is easy, they might engage in "a little white lie" such as "We'll get back to you." What might happen if you could stop "selling" and start listening? What impact would that have on building "trust" with your prospect, leading to getting the real truth on the table?

Problem Number 2: The Incumbent is Lying in Wait

The incumbent is the advisor who is currently providing your prospect investment products and services. And, trust me, this incumbent has a direct, active role to play in any prospect meeting—whether or not they are actually sitting at the table.

Let's suppose that you are in a meeting where you and the prospect immediately connect. Immediate rapport! She's speaking honestly to you about her needs and problems, and agrees that you can provide the solutions. You get the information you need to come back with a proposal and when you do, your ideas knock her socks off. Is the deal done?

Not yet. Somebody has to deal with the third party in this triangle: the incumbent advisor. And, because most people hate dispensing bad news and will do anything they can to avoid a confrontation, she isn't going to pick up the phone and tell her friendly, home-town advisor to just "hit the road, Jack!"

No, she is going to tell her incumbent advisor that she has received a very comprehensive proposal and her family is thinking about making a change. When she does, her advisor will come flying in the door before her phone even has a chance to cool off, and ask for a last look. He will get it and then take your proposal back to his firm and return with an offer designed to get her to do the easiest thing in the world—nothing.

As the new advisor, you are advocating change. Change is hard. The old, familiar advisor—with essentially the same fee structure and similar service—wants the prospect to do nothing. Doing nothing, not making a change is the easiest way out for your prospect.

All of a sudden, instant rapport becomes immediate rejection. You've been "rolled," the incumbent got a last look and used the advantage of incumbency to block you out.

Getting "Rolled"

Getting rolled: When the incumbent advisor leverages the relationship to get the opportunity to see your ideas and match them – keeping the business!

An advisor told the story of having an outstanding meeting with a new prospect. The prospect was excited, impressed and interested. He used phrases like "We will definitely look into this," and "Your proposal is outstanding, I am almost certain we can work together."

The advisor left the meeting with the money practically jingling in his pocket, but when it came time to close…poof! The opportunity was gone. The prospect gave the advisor the usual "We're looking at it closely. Call me in a couple of weeks." Later, my trainee found out and told me what really happened:

"Not long after he left my office, my prospect was on the phone with his incumbent advisor, telling him my ideas. The incumbent—my competitor—said something like 'Yeah, that's a really good idea…if you don't mind the back-end costs that are coming along.'

"My prospect got nervous. 'What kind of back-end costs?' His pal, the incumbent, was more than happy to tell him. 'Well,' he said, 'it's kind of like the Yugo. Remember when that car first came out? Everyone saw the sticker price and was really impressed. The car looked good, had a nice paint job and a new body style and was incredibly cheap. Buyers soon discovered that it had high-maintenance costs and wasn't very dependable. That was a real problem.'

"After that, the deal had vaporized. It didn't matter how good my proposal was, because the incumbent was there to kill it after I left. That's when I learned you've got to do more than just have a better fee structure. You've got to eliminate the incumbent. If you don't, you'll get 'rolled.'"

My friend is right. You must have a strategy to deal with the incumbent, to reduce his credibility and the power of his solutions. Because if the prospect can't fire the incumbent, he isn't really a prospect. He's just wasting your time.

Be a Prophet! If you suspect your prospect is going to get a negative opinion about your product or service from a third party, bring it up. Tell him it is going to happen. It will take the sting out of it. Your prospect will be able to say to the incumbent advisor "I knew you would say that!"

The incumbent is always going to be there. He's never going to just disappear. You are trying to take money out of his pocket, and he's going to fight you to keep it. And in that fight, he's got the upper hand.

Was my friend really trying to sell the prospect an unreliable "Yugo" of a deal? No, but the prospect knew the incumbent. As a businessperson, he knew exactly how good (or bad) the service was that he was getting at the time. Change is difficult, it involves risk and effort. So, when the incumbent raised even the most unsubstantiated doubts about the new advisor, the easiest thing in the world for the prospect to do was nothing. And if you're an incumbent, clients who do nothing are the best kind to have.

There's no question about it, the incumbent is going to try to roll you and to prevail you'll need a strategy to prevent it. In Chapter 11, you will learn a technique that is guaranteed to increase your chances of winning (CBO & SRU) by 80%! You'll learn proven, tested strategies to overcome the incumbent advisor's advantage, close the deal, and win.

So, What Do I Do Now?

Let's recap the real situation you face every day as you try to "sell."

- In virtually every prospect meeting, there is an incumbent advisor occupying your space.

- If the prospect can't fire the incumbent, he/she is not a prospect.

- The prospect wants to speak honestly to you about his/her business, but you have to get out of the way.

- When you are "selling," you are learning nothing that can help you break the incumbent's relationship with the prospect.

Therefore, you have little chance of success.

Pretty clear problem, right? So what's the solution?

The solution is to stop selling and start winning. You can do this by developing a strategy that deals directly with each of these problems. You can learn how to drive a "wedge" between the prospect and the incumbent, to create space between the prospect and his incumbent advisor. You can learn to use that space to beat the incumbent and win.

I've developed a strategy that can do just that. It's called "The Wedge," and once you learn it, you will never have to "sell" again.

Chapter 2

The Two Problems That Keep You "Selling"

Problem #1: The Incumbent

The single most important concept I have learned in my years as a sales coach and trainer is this: *Until you have a strategy to deal with the incumbent, you don't have a prospect.*

The incumbent is the person currently providing your prospect with investment products and services. And, almost every time you meet with a prospect or write a proposal, the incumbent advisor is a key player.

Why? Because of the laws of physics:

No Two Objects Can Occupy The Same Space At The Same Time

Unless you have an unusual niche that you've chosen to concentrate on, it's a certain bet that someone else provides investment products and services similar to yours. And, unless you're talking with a family with very new investable assets, chances are, there is someone providing your services to the prospects you meet with. That provider—your competition—is the incumbent advisor.

The incumbent is occupying the space you need, and as long as he is there, you cannot win (CBO & SRU). Many prospects are willing to meet with you. A meeting with you is a great way to get a briefing on new products or services available in the marketplace. This information is certainly worth an hour of their time and the price of a cup of coffee.

However, you can be confident of one thing: Before the prospect ever makes a change, he is going to go to his incumbent—the person currently occupying your space—to get a "counter-opinion," in a sense giving him a last look at whatever proposal you put together. After all, the incumbent is the current service provider. He has a standing relationship with your prospect. It is the most natural thing in the world for him, therefore, to be given a chance to share his opinion and match your offer.

Unless you have a strategy to deal with that fact, the incumbent will put together a proposal which is similar to yours. He'll present it with enough passion to convince your prospect, his client, that there is no need for a change, in a sense cut you out. Who likes change anyway?

Congratulations, you've just been "rolled." All of your work, all of your ideas, all of your time has been wasted. Why? Because you never had a prospect to start with, you just had someone to sell to.

An Object At Rest Tends To Stay At Rest

By definition, when you are pitching a prospect, you are asking him to make a change. Change is difficult and consumes precious time and energy. It is always easier to do nothing…which is exactly what the incumbent wants.

No matter how well-known your firm is, no matter what its reputation, when you ask a prospect to end a long-standing relationship with the incumbent, you are asking him to take a chance. Your firm may have been around for 50 years, but not for the prospect.

The person who has been there for the prospect is that familiar face, the person who sends a gift basket every Thanksgiving, the incumbent. And you want him to break up that relationship.

So, when you present an option that saves the prospect 20% on taxes, or might improve the return, he may be tempted to jump on it. But in fact, the best solution for him (from an inertia standpoint) would be to have the same deal provided by his friendly old incumbent. So what does the prospect do? He calls the incumbent, of course!

The incumbent will stop by, sit across the desk as he has done so many times before, and remind the prospect how good things are right now.

"Now, Joe," the incumbent will say, "we've known each other for 10 years. I'd hate to see you do something that jeopardizes all the work we've done together preparing for your retirement.

Before you go and do anything rash, let me talk to my staff and see what we can get done here. I can't promise we'll match everything, but we'll make it so easy for you, that it wouldn't make sense to do anything differently."

And, unless you have a strategy to deal with it, that's exactly what Joe the Prospect will do. The incumbent will put together a deal that is "good enough." It will be close enough to yours to allow the prospect to justify doing what he *wants* to do...nothing.

The prospect's desire to do nothing is a force of nature that gives the incumbent advisor an advantage over you in every deal—even if the advisor is lousy. That's why you need a plan to overcome that advantage before you even sit down with the prospect.

For Every Action, There Is An Equal And Opposite Reaction

For too many advisors, the solution to the incumbent advisor is to "push." "Pushing" is a classic symptom of selling.

By pushing, I mean going on the attack, demeaning the incumbent, demonstrating why someone would have to be an idiot to keep that firm over your own. The prospect, who has in fact done just that, will get your message loud and clear. And if you don't want someone to become defensive and dishonest, you shouldn't talk negatively about the choices they've made. For example a statement like, "Wow, I can't believe your advisor placed you in this fund!?" will not win you the business.

Millions of professionals have said that it is unprofessional to trash your competition. That is very true, but is that the real reason most people don't do it? Probably not, the real reason is that it doesn't work.

Why? Because nobody wants to be told they're stupid. And if I'm the prospect, and I hired the current advisor, and you tell me what a lousy decision that was, you're not only attacking the incumbent, you're also demeaning my ability to make decisions. I'm sitting behind my desk, and you walk in, insinuating that I've made bad decisions, and then you ask me to do you a favor and buy from you? You've got to be kidding!

That's why it's a mistake to jump on the prospect's first indication of dissatisfaction, like a shark attacking a wounded swimmer. While your goal is to drive a wedge between the prospect and the incumbent advisor, if you attack, the prospect will feel like you are making *him* look bad for making the wrong choice. The harder you attack (your action), the more defensive the prospect will become (his equal and opposite reaction).

Never attack your competitors. Let the prospect do it!

Once again, this is simple human nature. People don't like to acknowledge their mistakes, and making that mistake more obvious doesn't make them feel any better about it. Therefore, your difficult task is to help the prospect reveal his dissatisfaction with his incumbent advisor, but without making him feel defensive. You want the prospect to ask you to help him make a change, not get into an argument about whether or not he needs to make one. That is why you need an incumbent strategy for every prospect.

Problem #2: Honest, Open Dialogue

The other major problem that keeps you selling instead of winning is the prospect's unwillingness to be transparent and vulnerable and tell you the truth. This unwillingness is what keeps your (incumbent) competitors alive, and you "dead on arrival."

Let's return to the laws of physics. Here is the situation:

1. The incumbent is occupying your space.

2. Inertia is keeping him there.

3. If you start pushing the prospect by attacking the incumbent, the prospect is likely to perceive it as an attack against him and start pushing back.

What you need to overcome these conditions, is what Sir Isaac Newton would have called "an outside force."

That outside force is the prospect's own dissatisfaction with the incumbent. That dissatisfaction may be clearly evident to the prospect before you even show up, or it may be buried in the back of his mind. It could simply be that the prospect thinks his incumbent advisor is doing a good job because he has no idea that it can be done better.

Whatever the source, if there is dissatisfaction, frustration, disappointment, or concern—I use the term "pain" to describe all of these—that "pain" can be used to drive a wedge between the prospect and the incumbent. The emotional power of this pain is the outside force that can overcome the incumbent's position and move him out of the picture.

Pain is absolutely essential to your success if you want to break apart incumbent relationships and win (CBO & SRU). But to find it, you need an honest, open rapport with the prospect.

People Always Find A Way To Do What They Really Want To

This is a *key* point: People will find a way to justify doing what they want to do. And in many cases, what people want to do is eliminate risk in their lives and often times the best way to do that is to do "nothing". I've seen hundreds of situations where an advisor brings in a proposal that was clearly better than the incumbent's, but the prospect wouldn't make a change…simply because they didn't want to. The best proposal didn't get it done. Once again, the incumbent held the trump card.

How can you get the prospect to want to make the change? An essential step is to make contact, to create a level of rapport that allows the prospect to tell you what he is really trying to accomplish and what his true needs are. When the prospect is comfortable with you and is confident that you can help him accomplish his goals, he will want to work with you, and the dynamics will begin to change. Remember, if the prospect wants to work with you, he will find a way to do so.

The Power Of "Columbo"

One way to look at the Wedge is as a way to use emotional energy to overcome the incumbent's advantage. However, this depends heavily on the prospect's willingness to explore his or her own emotions, to talk honestly about what he or she wants to accomplish, and to feel comfortable sharing that information with you.

The wrong approach is to sell, to demonstrate how much you know, to ignore what the prospect has to say, and try too hard to convince, persuade, and influence your way to a sale. Lecturing the prospect and attacking the incumbent are techniques which are commonly used in sales, but they don't help the prospect on his path of self-discovery.

Instead, I suggest you use the power of "Columbo."

Do you remember the TV show starring Peter Falk as Detective Columbo? Falk's "Columbo" was hardly an impressive figure. From a sales standpoint, he was a disaster; poorly dressed, unshaven, disheveled, and disorganized. His conversations meandered far away from the "features and benefits" type of dialogue we've been taught to use.

Instead, Columbo was kind of a dumpy-looking guy who was hardly intimidating. His suspects (particularly the guilty ones) often told him the truth unintentionally, because he was so unassuming, so non-threatening, and so genuinely curious. The result was that Columbo would solve the problem at hand every week in an hour—counting commercial breaks.

Childlike Curiosity

When my daughter Kendall was young, she found things out the same way. She would often walk up to me and ask me a question and when she did, she'd kind of tilt her head and get this look on her face that said, "I'm really curious, I really care, and I want to know the answer." Because she was so sincere, I would give her answers to difficult questions that, to be honest, sometimes surprised myself. Like Columbo, there was nothing threatening in the questions, so the answers came easily and honestly.

Find The Pain and Win (CBO & SRU)

By establishing this dialogue, you will create a climate that promotes truth-telling and honesty. You will need that honesty to find the pain, hurts, wants and needs that allow you to drive The Wedge.

We will talk more about the tactics used to set up The Wedge in the next section of the book. First, let me demonstrate why discovering the prospect's dissatisfaction (or "pain", as we call it) is absolutely vital to Driving The Wedge, busting up incumbent relationships and winning (CBO & SRU).

Fix It Or Forget It

In his outstanding book *Solution Selling*, Michael Bosworth points out that when people have a problem, they either fix it or forget it. For example, what would your company do if your accountant kept getting the math wrong and wasting company money? Why, they would fire him, of course! That's a direct "fix the pain" model.

Problem…Incompetent accountant

Result…Pain in my pocketbook

Solution…Fire him/her and get someone competent

However, not all of life's problems are that easy to fix. Your firm, for example, may want an accountant who not only gets the numbers right, but also supplies weekly reports that are comprehensive, easy-to-read, and make economic forecasts about your company's revenues too.

Not surprisingly, you may try several accountants and never find one whose work is completely satisfactory or who can help your company achieve its goals. Your firm may conclude that the level of service you want simply is not available and eventually settle on an accountant whose work is not completely satisfactory. The conclusion may be that this is just one of the insoluble problems of business and not worth wasting any more time on.

Latent Memory Stores Forgotten Problems

In these cases, the dissatisfaction or "pain," as we will call it, is latent. Prospects don't wake up every morning and say, "Why can't I get my reports on time?" They just accept that timely reports are not available and carry on. The human mind does not like insoluble problems. It either finds an answer or forgets the problem, which is then stored in latent memory.

In an ideal world, every prospect will be sitting in his or her office when you arrive sighing "Thank God you're here! I've been looking for someone who can finally produce statements like I want them!" But that rarely happens. Instead, you must help your prospects along the path of self-discovery to uncover the latent "pain" they have forgotten.

If you can get your prospect to connect with you in an open and honest way, you can ask questions that can spur his or her latent memory and bring the pain to the forefront. To do so, your prospect has to believe that you might be able to do something about it, and be convinced that you can be told this information without fear that you will use it against him or her.

Prospects Raise Walls

The prospect's fear—that the salesperson will "use my pain against me to try and force me into a decision I don't want to make"—is the primary reason why prospects raise walls of dishonesty and insincerity with salespeople. This is one reason why the "sales shark" approach used by aggressive salespeople often fails. The prospect is the one with the problem, and he wants to be in charge of implementing the solution. He certainly doesn't want to be pressured and berated by salespeople—even when they're right.

However, when you can overcome this fear and create an open, honest dialogue, you have the opportunity to jog the prospect's latent memory and bring up some of that unresolved pain. If the prospect is comfortable with you and believes you can be useful, he will share this pain with you, giving you the opportunity to drive the Wedge.

The Wedge At Work

The Wedge is a universal process that is effective for anyone wanting to win new business, no matter what industry. Here is a sample conversation between a prospect and a salesperson representing a computer networking company. In it, you will see how pain is discovered, and then how it is used to drive the Wedge. (The comments in parentheses are the individual elements of The Wedge for reference later in the book.)

Salesperson: "About a year ago, I was working with the president of a company much like yours. One of his greatest concerns was the hassle and cost of borrowing money while waiting to collect his receivables. What he said he wanted was to reduce the time between shipping the product and getting paid. We were able to help him with that and as a result, he's reduced his lag time by 11 days and his costs of borrowing money are down 67%....Tell me about your situation."

Prospect: "We've tried to accomplish the same thing. Our biggest challenge has been to get the information from our system to produce the invoices quickly." (**Note:** Anytime the prospect throws us a concern, we think of it as a softball and want to play catch. So we throw it back. Anytime a prospect throws you a "softball," it is the basis of a **"Reactive Wedge."**)

Salesperson: "When you told the people you're dealing with that you weren't happy with the information from your system and that you wanted them to speed it up, I'm curious: What did they say?"

Prospect: "They said they would try to get us better and faster information."

Salesperson: "How's that going so far?" (This is **"Check Pulse."**)

Prospect: "Nothing has really changed, I'm afraid."

Salesperson: "And, you're OK with that" (said in a very low tone, very laid back). (This is **"Take Away."**)

Prospect: "Not exactly. We have some significant dollars tied up in there."

Salesperson: "Let me ask you this: When your current service provider came out and conducted a time-line analysis, and they looked at billing sources, how the information flows to your billing department, the speed with which invoices go out, and the time it takes for those bills to be paid by your customers and to get that revenue into your system so that you could find the quickest path to get your cash back in and reduce your out-of-pocket expenses, were you comfortable with how they went through that process?" (This is **"Picture Perfect"** part of a **"Proactive Wedge."**)

Prospect: "Actually, uh, they didn't do that. To my knowledge, they don't even know how long it takes right now or the impact of turning that information around more quickly."

Salesperson: "Well, I don't suppose it's caused any real financial burden" (laid back, simple statement). (**Take-Away.**)

Prospect: "Yes, it has. In fact, we pay them a lot of money to do the best work possible. They should've handled this already."

Salesperson: "Well, can we talk about that?"

Prospect: "Sure."

Salesperson: "With regard to your billing and cash flow, what would you like to have happen?" (This is **"Vision Box."**)

Prospect: "Much like what you were talking about, I would like to cut our borrowing costs and the key to that is getting our billing out faster and reducing our collection time."

Salesperson: "Tell me, how much faster do you see as reasonable, and what effect do you believe that would have on your borrowing costs?"

Prospect: "I'm not really sure. I think it would be significant."

Salesperson: "OK, let's talk about how you see that happening. Would you want someone to do an analysis, a time-line of what is happening now?"

Prospect: "Yes, that makes sense to me."

Salesperson: "OK, whom do you see involved in a project like this?"

Prospect: "I'd want Joe, he's our Finance Manager, and Sally, our I.S. Manager, and Jane in Operations."

Salesperson: "So, what I hear you saying is that what you need to get your revenue up is a computer system and strategy that will get reports out as soon as invoices come in, and that will also track those reports along with their status until the money comes in. Am I on the right track?" (This is **"Replay."**)

Prospect: "Yes, that is what we'd like to have happen!"

Salesperson: "OK, well there's your game plan, what would you like me to do?

Prospect: "I'd like to get a proposal".

Salesperson: "OK, putting together a proposal is the easy part. Can we talk about the hard part?"

And from there you go into the REHEARSAL process to determine up front, before you invest a significant amount of time in putting together a proposal, if they can say goodbye to the other guy in order to get what they want!

Conclusion

As you can see, The Wedge deals directly with the problem of the incumbent, but it depends a great deal on the establishment of an honest rapport between you and your prospect. This honesty is essential if you are going to get the prospect to acknowledge his pain, and it also allows you to collaborate on specific solutions to specific problems the prospect must solve to achieve his goals.

Focusing on the prospect's goals is an essential part of moving away from "selling" and into winning. Focusing on the incumbent is also an important element because until the incumbent is dealt with, you cannot achieve your own goal of winning. In fact, one could argue that the entire difference between "selling" and winning is in *your* focus. (CBO & SRU)

When you focus on yourself and your firm and you go into a prospect meeting just slinging your best pitch, you are selling.

When you focus on your prospect and how you can help him achieve his goals by solving a specific problem, when you walk into the prospect meeting prepared to anticipate those problems and develop specific solutions, then you start winning. (CBO & SRU)

So, What Do I Do Now?

A quick recap:

- There are two problems that selling cannot solve:

    o   The presence of the incumbent

    o   The prospect's unwillingness to talk to you honestly about his situation

- When it comes to dealing with the incumbent, The Laws of Physics are working against you:

    o   No two objects can occupy the same space at the same time.

    o   An object at rest tends to stay at rest.

    o   For every action, there is likely to be an equal and opposite reaction.

- To overcome these conditions, you must bring an outside force to bear on the prospect/incumbent relationship. That force is the prospect's pain.

- "Pain" is short-hand for the dissatisfaction the prospect has with the service he is currently receiving from the incumbent advisor, or for the desire the prospect has for a higher level of performance that has not yet been achieved.

- The Wedge works by helping prospects discover for themselves their dissatisfaction, and then determining that you have the ability to resolve this "pain" and help them achieve more success for themselves and their families.

- Latent Memory is that part of your brain upon which those things you've surrendered to or have accepted as is lie in a dormant state.

Now that you understand the general concepts of The Wedge and what makes it work, the next three chapters will show you the techniques to use to create the right climate for using The Wedge in real life. If you will learn these specific techniques, you will have more opportunities to drive The Wedge, break incumbent relationships and give yourself the opportunity to win (CBO & SRU)—which means more revenue and additional assets to manage.

Chapter 3

Knowing What You Don't Know: How To Find, Analyze, and Use Research To Turn Even the Toughest Prospect Into a Client

"It's not what you know, and it's not who you know, either. It's what you know about who you know that counts."

— *Anonymous*

If you are like a lot of advisors, you spend most of your time on the go. You're on the street, generating leads, making calls, dropping in on potential clients, and servicing your existing clients. You leave home early and come in late. You spend more time talking into your cell phone then you do to your family.

This approach allows very little time to find out much about your prospects. And it doesn't even acknowledge the existence of the number one deal-breaker, the incumbent. There is no strategy to put you, the advisor, into an advantageous position against the incumbent, thereby increasing your odds of collecting bigger checks.

For people who are selling, The Wedge is problematic because it forces you to slow down. It requires that you find out about both the prospect *and* the incumbent. It also requires that you do the research so you can meet your prospective client with a game plan that will improve your chances of getting hired.

In every sales game there are three primary players that need to be researched thoroughly:

- Your prospect

- Your competition (incumbent advisor)

- You

Easier said than done, yes? Research isn't easy, and it can be time-consuming. However, before you become discouraged, consider the many sources of quality information now available to you:

- Your firm and co-workers

- Vendors who serve you

- Your other clients

- The media: the Internet, news clippings, the library, etc.

The easiest thing for you to do before calling on a prospect is to search the local paper's Internet archives for the recent news stories mentioning the prospect's name or business. Think of the impact you can make on a new prospect by quoting a comment he/she made in a recent interview in the business section.

This information, and mountains more, is readily available on your computer at the click of a mouse. Internet research absolutely must be part of your preparation for prospect meetings.

The Most Important Research Tool

The most important research tool is not a computer, a library, or a friend who will dig through the prospect's trash can. *The most valuable tool is your willingness to ask for help.* Information is everywhere, if you look. The more quality information you have, the easier it is to drive The Wedge between your prospect and their incumbent advisor.

Researching The Incumbent

When researching a prospect and their business, one of the most important questions you want to answer is "Who is sitting in my chair?" With any financial product, it's almost a certainty that there is an incumbent advisor in place. Knowing who that is, and the broker dealer they work for, seems like common sense.

But it isn't. I'm astonished at the number of advisors who meet with prospects and have no idea who is already sitting in *their* chair. That would be like your favorite sports team playing a game tonight and not knowing who they're matching up against.

Finding out who the incumbent is should not be a problem. In investments, as in most industries, there are a relative handful of top competitors and you probably know who they are! Amazingly, however, very few sales organizations keep up-to-date information on their competitors. It is very rare for me to go into a coaching session where the advisors keep an active file on the people who compete with them for business. Keep this in mind; EVERY TIME you meet with a new prospect, you not only get clues, you get real evidence about how they serve clients.

One advisor friend of mine, who is in the top 0.5% in production at his firm, Drew Watson, told me this story:

"When I know a client is coming from one of my competitors that I've done my homework on, I can predict what they'll have on their statement when they show it to me. Like Carnac the Great, the old Johnny Carson routine, I'll hold the envelope to my head and predict with great accuracy what investments they are holding. The client is generally in awe that I'm able to predict 80-90% of the investments they own as well as show them why they are dissatisfied with these investments as I interpret the research (i.e. stock overlap, overweight in asset category, high expenses, etc.)."

That is knowing your competition, and that builds credibility. So at the risk of being repetitive, let me remind you again: The Number One deal-breaker in every deal is the incumbent. As long as the incumbent controls "the chair," you don't really have a prospect. You cannot get hired until you break the incumbent relationship, and the competing advisor is going to do everything possible to prevent that.

If you don't know anything about the firms you're competing against, if you don't know what they offer or anything about their fee structure, if you don't even know where they're located, you're not in a position to win (CBO & SRU).

How can you research your competitors? Once again, start with your team. They are competing against them every day. Ask your fellow advisors about previous experiences they've had competing against the incumbent in question, successful and otherwise.

You will want to create a common file for clippings, brochures, previous proposals, client statements, and other information about competitors that you and your team come across. The process of gathering this information is valuable in and of itself because it focuses you on the third party—the incumbent.

When researching an incumbent, you want to know who they are, what they do, how long they have been the incumbent, and how they were able to get in. What is the nature of their relationship with the prospect? Is the prospect just a customer, buying from the incumbent the same way they buy bread at the store? Or is the prospect one of the incumbent's friends, someone they have a close, partner-like relationship with?

Researching Yourself To Find Your Advantage

My company, The Wedge Group, conducted a marketing research project on investment firms and made an interesting discovery. With almost no exception, all those we contacted marketed their firm in an identical manner emphasizing the following features: innovative financial products, outstanding service, on-line tools, experience, highly-trained staff, and a solid reputation. Every firm claimed that these features made them different from their competitors.

At the conclusion of our research, I made the determination that the so-called "marketing efforts" used by most of these firms were failing because what they thought were their strengths were really the minimum acceptable standards for being in business. In other words, what these firms thought made them "better" really made them the same as everybody else.

When we looked at the major investment companies, we found that they were to a great degree offering the same services and products at competitive fees. The advisory firms representing these major investment companies were in fact representing even more sameness.

The service, people, and products that they boast are "Excellence," have become the minimum standard for business in America's competitive workplace. Meeting these standards has turned every advisor into a cheerleader for the same quality level of products and services.

What does this mean to you? It means that if you're selling features and benefits, you're losing, because dozens of your competitors are working the same prospects and selling the same things in the same way. And if you and the incumbent are essentially the same, why should the prospect go through the pain of making a change?

This is where researching your own firm becomes vitally important. Chances are you and your competitors are offering very similar products and services. The difference isn't in what you do, but how you do it. *It isn't your products' features or benefits you need to sell, but how you deliver those products and services in a way that makes a difference for the prospect.*

Your challenge is to research what you do and how you do it in order to find your strengths. Once you do that, you'll be prepared when you meet with a prospect to compare your strengths to your competition's weaknesses.

Strength vs. Weakness

You are in a game against your competitor, the incumbent, a game that you want to win (CBO & SRU). The incumbent advisor only has to tie, or may even be able to score a little less, because he has a relationship with the prospect that you don't have.

If you haven't compared your strengths against the incumbent's weaknesses in advance, what's going to happen? You may mention the area of well-trained staff, for example, only to find out that the incumbent's staff is equally well trained. Your strength vs. his strength: It's a wash. And since, as they say in baseball, "a tie goes to the runner," you lose.

You may demonstrate clearly that you have a fast turn-around time, only to find out that the incumbent is faster. Your weakness vs. his strength: You lose again.

What you need to do, as the new advisor competing against the incumbent, is to match your strengths vs. his or her weaknesses. That is the only winning match-up where you have the advantage.

You		Incumbent	Result
Strength	vs.	Strength	Wash (You lose)
Weakness	vs.	Strength	You Lose
Strength	vs.	Weakness	Your Advantage

The Dallas Cowboys have a Wide Receiver named Terrell Owens, who is considered one of the better Wide Receivers in football. At the same time, the Denver Broncos have 2006 Defensive MVP Champ Bailey as their Corner Back .

The results are interesting. When Dallas and Denver play, the best players on the field never help their teams win, because the best vs. the best results in a wash. The games are won by players who are not as good as Owens or Bailey, but who have more favorable match-ups.

Most advisors work for firms that do essentially the same things. Therefore, although it is hard, you must find *how* what you do is different. This may seem like a strange concept, but before you meet with a prospect, it's vital that you know what you do well, how you do it, what kinds of problems you can solve, and how quickly. You need to be prepared to focus your conversation with the prospect on areas where you and your company are strong and the competition is weak.

If you match your competitors feature for feature, service for service, you will lose because you can never offer the one exclusive product the incumbent possesses: an existing relationship with the prospect.

The incumbent has one. You don't.

To break apart that incumbent relationship, you must put your strength against the incumbent's weakness. This is why research is vitally important.

Without it, how will you know which services and products to promote when you meet with the prospect? How else can you make strategic decisions before your prospect meeting so you can drive The Wedge which will give you the winning (CBO & SRU) advantage?

The Real Test Of Your Research

Check your calendar for your next scheduled prospect meeting and ask yourself these questions:

- Who will make the final decision to hire me?

- Who do I know that knows these people?

- Do my fellow advisors know anyone who knows these people?

- What are the most common problems for this type of client?

- What are the specific problems or issues that my prospect is trying to address?

- Who is the incumbent advisor?

- What are the three things I do better than the incumbent?

- What questions can I ask the prospect that will help him see clearly that we are the better choice?

- What are the three things my firm and I do better than anyone else?

These are just a few of the questions you should have concrete, rehearsed answers to before you walk into a prospect meeting. There are many more, and I urge you to develop your own list of "what's important."

The key question on research is this: Do you have a strategy to win the research game? Until you do, you are fighting a losing battle. Your time, effort, and research can guarantee you an opportunity to get hired, if you have the winning "Wedge."

Recap

- You must research: yourself, your prospects, and the incumbent

- It's not what you do, but how you do it.

- It's what you do that your competition doesn't do that leads to where your prospect is underserved by the incumbent.

- Strength vs. Strength is a wash—you lose!

Chapter 4

Rapport: Creating An Environment For "Truth-Telling"

One of the two great challenges facing every advisor is the prospect's unwillingness to tell the "whole" truth. There are several reasons why, not the least of which is the fact that by suggesting he make a change, you are challenging a previous decision. The quickest way to get people to be defensive is to tell them that the decisions they've made were wrong.

Therefore, before you meet with a new prospect, you need a strategy that you can use to create a climate of truthfulness in your meeting. You want to make it easy for the prospect to be honest about his or her situation, goals, and even his or her mistakes. It won't be easy.

Before a prospect will be honest with you, he or she must be comfortable with you and believe that you are able to help. *These are the two tests: credibility and comfort.* Until you pass these two tests, it is unlikely that you will have an open, honest dialogue with the people you meet with.

When I am training people to use The Wedge, I refer often to Michael Brooks' book, *Instant Rapport,* for strategies that will create an environment in which the prospect is *willing* to tell you the truth. Rapport helps you quickly create a relationship based on comfort and credibility. You want your prospect to be comfortable speaking with you honestly, and you want him to believe that if he tells you his problem, you can do something about it.

Taking this approach, you can see that the entire burden for creating effective communication is on you. It's your job to find out what you need to know. You can't count on the prospect to tell you. In a new prospect interview, you're the one who wants something; therefore, you are the one responsible for establishing rapport. You must be flexible and willing to make shifts in body posture and the speed and tone of your voice, as well as adjust your emotional state to match that of your prospect.

6 Reasons Why Prospects Don't Tell the "Whole" Truth

1. They don't like you.
2. They don't trust you.
3. They don't want to look stupid by admitting their mistake.
4. They have another relationship to protect.
5. They are on a "power trip" to compensate for low self esteem.
6. Your sales technique shows.

How To Establish Rapport

There is an old cliché that states, "When in Rome, do as the Romans do." What does that mean? Does it mean you need to dress like they dress, talk like they talk, sit like they sit, like what they like? Yes, to a great degree. What you will find to be true is that people like people who are most like themselves. The more two people share in common, the greater the degree of rapport.

Do different situations, people, or places make you feel at least a little uncomfortable? Of course they do. On the other hand, do you generally feel comfortable with that which you consider normal, or just like you? Most people do. So the question is, how do you consistently create an environment where people feel comfortable? One way is for you to mimic what is normal for them.

I was working with a young woman who had been in sales for about one year. She had been taught to always sit up straight as an arrow with both feet planted firmly on the floor. Her posture was so erect that she looked almost uncomfortable. In her new job, she was calling on small business owners of manufacturing facilities. She would go into a meeting all prim, proper, and professional to meet with a guy that didn't wear a tie and sat back in his chair a little slumped with one leg crossed over the other.

She already had a couple of strikes against her for being young and not having much in common with her prospects, but she accentuated those differences by the way she sat and talked. If her goal was to create an environment where her prospect felt comfortable and talked openly, she probably wasn't going to achieve that goal. So what could she have done differently?

Match and Mirror

There are many areas in which you can create rapport. One area is simply by talking about things that you and the prospect share in common. We call this "conscious" rapport, because you consciously make a decision to pick out something as a point of conversation such as a photo or picture hanging on the wall or an object on the prospect's desk. Even though the effort is obvious (conscious), it's a nice way to break the ice and form an area of commonality.

But what kind of effect is there on your prospect when you adjust the speed of your voice to match his or hers? What about when you adjust the way you sit to provide a mirror image of your prospect? The answer is *subconscious rapport*. By matching their voice, the speed and tone, as well as mirroring their body posture, your prospect will feel much more comfortable with you and not really know why. If asked, they would just say, I like him and felt comfortable with him. But they, more than likely, wouldn't know why.

These rapport strategies are powerful tools. They will enable your prospect to get comfortable with you more quickly, which will lead to a willingness to be more vulnerable and to talk about what is really important—his goals, dreams and desires for his family and for himself.

I once had a meeting with a gentleman almost 25 years my senior. He was a typical Texan, in that he talked with a drawl—kind of slow and easy going. We were having breakfast one morning at a hotel in Dallas and I began the conversation with a very active "Match and Mirror" strategy: slowing the speed of my voice down to match his, sitting back in my chair very relaxed, just like him. The comfort level was high, and the level of truth-telling was significant.

However, as the conversation progressed, I could see the opportunity for us to get a $700,000 contract that would generate a $70,000 fee for us. The more that fee became a reality, the more excited I became. This excitement (not to mention the effect of three cups of coffee) began to work against me.

I went from mirroring his posture and matching the speed and tone of his voice, to sitting up, leaning forward and talking faster. That response is normal for me, particularly when I am closing in on a $700,000 deal, but it wasn't normal for him. In fact, it nearly cost me the deal.

Why? The reason I had a great chance of getting that deal in the first place was because our intimate level of rapport had allowed him to talk openly about his current dissatisfaction, his "pain." He had problems that needed solutions. That was his emotional state.

Meanwhile, my emotional state had shifted to one of excitement. To him, it appeared that the longer he talked about his unhappiness, the happier I became. It took me a few minutes to notice, but as I was becoming excited, he was becoming turned off. I had mismatched his emotional state as well as his posture and voice. Where before there was harmony, there was now disharmony.

I finally noticed how his body posture had shifted away from me when I was sitting up. He seemed to cower a bit, as if to say: "Back off, buddy." When I recognized what was going on, I slowly, but deliberately, made a shift back to matching him. I sat back and slowed my voice from excited to matching his "concerned" state of mind, and then he made his shift. We were back in harmony and rapport was reestablished.

Here is an example of how "match and mirror" works in your own life. Have you ever had "one of those days?" You know, the days when, from the time you get up and stub your toe on the closet door until you come rushing into the office late after sitting in traffic all morning, nothing goes right? Maybe you're just in a foul mood, or you've forgotten your wife's birthday. Well, the only thing worse than "one of those days" is having it interrupted by "Happy Bob."

"Happy Bob" (or "Babs") is the person at your office whose core philosophy of life is that everybody should be happy. When "Happy Bob" encounters an unhappy co-worker, he feels like it's his job in life to cheer them up. He's always got a cartoon clipped out of some "Perky People" monthly magazine, or he's downloaded Letterman's Top 10 list from the night before. Whatever it takes, he wants you to be happy.

When you're in a good mood, Happy Bob is a pleasant enough person to be around. But on "one of those days," you want to grab his "Don't Worry, Be Happy!" paperweight and shove it down his throat. The mismatch of your emotional states can lead you to the brink of violence.

To a lesser degree, the same is true during a prospect meeting. People like people who are like themselves. If the person you are meeting is in a high-spirited, cheerful mood, raise your level to match it. However, if your prospect is much more reserved and quiet, don't try to make a party out of it. Match them and you will have much greater rapport.

Increasing your ability to establish a greater level of rapport by matching and mirroring is very important to getting out of the "selling" cycle and into the "winning" cycle. One of the primary keys to "winning" is quality information, the kind that can and will make the difference in the deal.

Travis Chaney, a great friend of mine and coach to many wildly successful advisors, recommends you identify the profile of your Top Shelf Clients. Consider people and businesses you want to work with most. This profile also includes such demographic factors as learning style, values, hobbies, age, community interests, etc. Great rapport building is much easier knowing that you are dealing with someone who shares similar traits and likes as you.

Creating Credibility

Matching and mirroring helps create rapport by creating comfort, by actively seeking paths of connection at the conscious and subconscious level. It is a pragmatic, easy-to-use technique that you can immediately put to work in your prospect meetings.

However, there is another essential element of truth-telling: credibility. Once again, the prospect must be comfortable enough to tell you the truth and believe you can help him once he tells you. Modeling will make him comfortable. How can you make yourself credible in his eyes? You can create credibility with a story.

Even if you've only done a minimal amount of research before your meeting, you should have a fairly accurate picture as to where the prospect's family is when you meet with them; what they are trying to achieve, and what problems they need to solve.

Regardless of the situation, you should be prepared with a powerful, well-rehearsed story regarding a third party that was in a situation similar to that of the prospect. This referral story should demonstrate that you have a clear understanding of the prospect, have worked with a similar situation to solve an important problem—one the prospect is likely to face—and that you are capable of doing the same today.

Stories work because they allow you to communicate without selling. When you're selling, you are either talking about yourself ("Our firm has been a leader in the industry for…") or you are cross-examining the prospect ("Have you ever had a problem with…"). Neither of these creates rapport or a climate for truth-telling. In fact, you are either boring the prospect by making the same pitch all of your competitors make, or you're possibly making him defensive about decisions made in the past.

Telling a story lets you share information about your competence and your firm without slinging sales talk at your prospect. It gives you a chance to demonstrate in very specific language how the products or services you offer have benefited people like the prospect, to let him "see you in action," if you will.

If you've done your research, you will be prepared with a story about a similar third party. An outline of such a story might look like this:

1. *"It's been my experience working with other clients…."* A broad outline of the current situation allows you to demonstrate your general familiarity with the marketplace.

2. *"A client I worked with was concerned about…."* A specific problem that you have helped solve for others and, based on your research, is likely to be a significant issue with this prospect.

3. *"When I spoke to one of my clients, what he wanted was…."* A solution to the problem listed previously.

4. *"We were able to…."* A simple statement that says "we gave him the solution."

5. *"As a result…."* List the concrete rewards in terms of time or money saved.

6. *"Now, tell me about your situation."* Find out about the prospect's situation.

You have now given the prospect a clear and specific scenario in which you helped a client in his situation solve a specific problem, and you did it in language that demonstrated your familiarity with his situation. You have immediately started establishing credibility. Your prospect now knows that you understand him/her and potential problems or concerns.

Moreover, when you started talking about the solutions your previous client wanted, you raised the question in your prospect's mind: "Are these solutions affordable or even doable?" By going next to "We gave them those solutions and, as a result, reduced their tax burden and saved time on implementation." you answered that question and raised another in the prospect's mind: "Can you do this for me?"

So, when you close with "Tell me about your situation," your prospect wants to talk about his current circumstances to get the answer to his question. You have accomplished your goal: the prospect wants to communicate and to do so honestly.

The goal of your story is clear: create comfort and establish credibility. The tactic is simple: tell a story that will resonate with the prospect, highlighting your proven ability to help other people like him solve their problems.

To recap, let's go over the credibility and triggering technique:

- State Concerns

- Solutions Wanted

- Solutions Given

- Give Positive Past Results

- Create credibility by showing that you understand your prospect and their potential concerns.

- Transform concerns into specific outcomes/solutions wanted.

- Create hope in prospect's mind: "If they solved it, maybe we can too."

- Quantify results in time or money saved. It needs to be concrete and specific.

- To create comfort and rapport, mirror and match body language, speed and tone of voice, and emotional state.

- To create credibility, use the story format above. BE CAREFUL— do not make the story all about you! It is intended to give your prospect something to relate to and at the same time build your credibility.

Chapter 5

Discovery: No Pain, No Change

So, you've done your research and you are more confident with your ability to fight the battles in areas where you have strengths and your competition has weakness. You now know more about your prospect and have a definitive path whereby you can make a real difference. You've sharpened your rapport building skills and have a strategy to encourage honest discussion with your prospect. Now you need to discover those issues that will motivate your prospect to make changes.

What is it you are looking for? In a word, pain.

Pain, loosely defined here as dissatisfaction, disappointment or unresolved tension, is an essential part of The Wedge. In fact, if you cannot find your prospect's pain, you will not be able to drive The Wedge, remove the incumbent and win (CBO & SRU). It truly is a case of "No pain, no change."

This is particularly true as a financial advisor. If you can't help your prospect identify and acknowledge dissatisfaction with his current advisor, you have virtually no chance of getting a shot at winning.

Even if you have a better offer, there is an 80% likelihood that your prospect will somehow give his current (the incumbent) advisor a chance to stay in the game by matching your offer. And in most cases, because it's cheaper to discount a little than it is to find a new customer, the incumbent advisor will match your fees, copy your ideas (or come close) and keep the business.

Remember, change is painful. If there is no pain, no dissatisfaction, no unfulfilled expectation, then why would a prospect want to go to the trouble of establishing a new relationship, taking a chance that things might even get worse over time? This is particularly true when, with a phone call or a meeting, they could probably use the competing advisor's proposal as leverage to get their existing advisor to do more for less.

So the million dollar questions are: "How do you find pain?" and "Where do you look?"

Finding The Pain

What makes an FBI investigator so good at finding the clues at the scene of the crime? He knows where to look. If they put you or me out there looking for clues we'd probably be going in circles in just moments. At the FBI Academy, they have a special course on how to find clues. In sales we should have a course on how to find pain, because that is the primary difference between "selling" and "winning".

A seller will go into a new business sales appointment ready to tell the company story. The winner will go into a new prospect interview, looking for the prospect's pain.

Where Does Pain Reside?

Think of your mind as a computer. The things you see on the screen of the computer represent the things in "the front of your mind," the immediate activity of the central processing unit of your computer. Just as your computer can only handle six or seven programs at a time, your active memory can only handle thinking about six or seven issues at once.

In addition to the central processing unit (CPU in computer lingo), your computer also has a hard drive, where it stores vast amounts of information and recall capacity. Millions of bytes of information sit dormant at all times, waiting for the right keystrokes to call them to the CPU and onto your screen into the computer's active memory.

This is a good analogy for what goes on inside our minds. Suppose it's Monday morning and you've got a meeting with a business owner at his office. Think for a moment what is happening when you walk into his office for that meeting. The business owner is usually up to his ears in activity: an employee quit that morning, the P&L just came out and needs to be reviewed, one of the kids has a soccer game at 5:30, and the printer just "ate" the report that is due tomorrow morning. His active memory is full of all these current events that are taking up space.

Now, if you happen to be in the business of solving one of these specific, immediate problems, you're in luck! You are likely to hear: "I'm glad you're here. I have this problem, can you help me?"

However, if your prospect doesn't have an immediate problem related to investments, planning for retirement, putting his kids through college, or protecting his estate from taxes, then you're going to have a difficult time getting his attention. So what do you do? You can ask the basic questions such as "Got any problems?" and "How are things going?", but you're unlikely to get a useful response.

This doesn't mean that there aren't any problems. It just means that you haven't pulled them up from the prospect's latent memory (his "hard drive") and into his active memory (onto the "screen"). The information is there, but hidden. You need the right set of "key strokes" or questions to bring it up and into the prospect's consciousness.

Fix It or Forget It

There are two human reactions when confronted with a problem: either find a solution—which involves the active memory—or set the problem aside until a satisfactory solution can be found—which means storing the problem in your latent memory. If you are capable of solving the problem, the problem is gone and the experience is mentally filed away as complete. On the other hand, if the problem cannot be solved for whatever reason—too expensive; no immediately definable solution; too much trouble, time, or effort—then the problem is forgotten, filed away in your latent memory.

So all of life's unsolved problems are stored in the latent memory. As an advisor, you have to know what those problems are likely to be and have a solution if you expect to reach your prospects at this level.

How Do You Know What Someone's
Problem Is Until You Ask?

Problems are like center stripes in the highway—they repeat themselves. If you have found a common problem among clients, it is reasonable to expect that most of your prospects will share the same problem. Although you won't know for sure until you ask, you can make that assumption and, if it calls up a reaction from the prospect's latent memory, confirm your assumption.

Some examples of the kinds of problems that people tend to store in their latent memory might include baldness, fear of public speaking, being over-weight, or having poor eyesight. On a day-to-day basis, if you asked these people how they are doing, they would respond "Fine, just fine!" If you asked if they had any personal problems they needed help with, they would likely say no.

But imagine if you mentioned to your friend with male pattern baldness that you had just found a product that grew hair instantly, what would be the response? "Really? You found a cure for baldness?"

Five minutes ago, he had no problems. Everything was fine. Now you are about to become a hero. Why? The problem was always there, but you presented the possibility of a solution.

Creating Pain
(The Proactive Wedge)

When you meet with a prospect who, even after rapport is established, does not share any pain with you, don't be fooled into thinking all of his problems have been solved. There are often times when it will seem the prospect isn't looking for solutions because he does not perceive that he has a problem. This doesn't mean things are perfect, far from it. It is just as likely that the prospect believes that things are as good as they're going to get, that the problems he faces are like the weather-conditions that must be dealt with but cannot be changed.

This prospect is in the "forget it" stage. Ongoing problems that could not be solved have been relegated to his latent memory. Since a person's active memory can only remember approximately seven items at the same time, it stores intractable or seemingly unsolvable problems in latent memory.

Thus the strategy you develop before you meet with the prospect isn't to "create" pain, but to uncover unresolved problems from the prospect's latent memory. This is the purpose of the "Proactive Wedge."

One important element for uncovering pain in the latent memory is using the "Picture Perfect" technique. We will cover "Picture Perfect" in more detail in Chapter 7, but from a preparation standpoint, your goal is to enter the meeting with a clear, well-conceived image of the ideal circumstances under which the prospect could be doing business, one that you can provide. You want to paint a word picture of perfection itself, of how things could be working for the prospect.

Here's a rather sexist example: Let's say you're married and you're talking to another married friend. What kind of a response do you think you would get if you said: "You know, I like being married, don't you? Don't you like how on Friday afternoon when you come home after a hard week's work, your wife meets you at the door with a big kiss and a tray with a cold beer, a bag of peanuts, and the remote control? Then she ushers you back to your favorite chair where she sits you down and pops your favorite movie into the DVD player, so you can get a few moments of relaxation and escape. I'm curious, are you comfortable with the way she greets you at the door?"

The answer you're likely to get back is: "What planet do you live on? I'm lucky if my wife is even there when I get home. Are you serious? Does your wife really do that?"

You've just created space between the incumbent and the prospect by getting the prospect to see the difference between what he has and what he *could* have. You've sown the seeds of dissatisfaction: the beginning of a Proactive Wedge.

You should enter each prospect meeting with several examples of "Picture Perfect" service which can be used to bring up unresolved or unrealized dissatisfaction. Obviously, you will be looking for reactive acknowledgments of pain, but you can't just hope to get lucky. You will have to develop your own strategies to create pain, to give yourself opportunity after opportunity to Drive the Wedge.

You want to enter your meetings thoroughly prepared and researched, and you want to create a credible, comfortable climate for the prospect to share any of the problems he's got in the front of his mind with you. You always want to look for reactive pain and a Reactive Wedge.

However, it's possible that there may not be any. That's when Proactive Wedges become useful. Proactive Wedges are educated guesses about what the prospect's concerns and problems are likely to be. They raise issues that, from your research, you would reasonably expect to give rise to dissatisfaction on the part of a prospect.

Here's an example for Investing. You are talking to a prospect about your previous work for a similar family, and you bring up the issue of risk.

> **Advisor:** "…and that's what he wanted, to feel more secure and have more control over his future. By the way, when your advisor met with you early in the relationship to lay out a stock selection process, and they got out reports with S&P ratings, dividend announcements, the stocks' relative strength, and whether stocks were over or under bought, so you could pick the most appropriate stocks. And so you wouldn't have to worry about buying underperforming securities and compromise your retirement plans. Were you comfortable with that process?

> **Prospect:** "Uh, they didn't do that. They just told me they have some really talented guys on staff to help with that."

> **Advisor:** OK. And you're satisfied with that!

> **Prospect:** Not really. I can't really justify why my money is where it is. It feels a little risky to me.

> **Advisor:** OK. Well can I put that on the shelf for a moment and let me ask you this.

> **Prospect:** Yeah, go ahead.

> **Advisor:** When your advisor comes out on a quarterly basis to rebalance your portfolio, gets out your financial plan with recommended asset allocation along with your account summary, compares the two to

determine where you're out of balance and then make the corrections. so you won't have to worry about too much risk and losing value in your portfolio or too little risk and losing return, how does that go?

Prospect: I only see my advisor once a year. I don't believe we've ever really done that.

Advisor: OK. And you don't see that as a big deal.

Prospect: Well, yes I do...

Now you've begun the Wedge Process.

Notice that this script assumes that the prospect never mentioned any problems, and that, if you had asked the question: "Are you satisfied with your agent's service," the answer would likely have been positive.

What the Proactive Wedge does is to assume that the prospect has unstated concerns (latent memory) (a fairly safe assumption) and then present a scenario of "Picture Perfect" service that would solve the problem. If the prospect has had these problems, you will jog his latent memory and he should be very interested in what you present. If he doesn't, you can go onto another Proactive Wedge and get another opportunity to find pain and remove the incumbent.

Chapter 6

Differentiation:
How You Do What You Do,
Better Than Anyone Else

I was doing a training session recently, when an enthusiastic young advisor who had just gotten into the business, made an astonishingly obvious, but important observation in front of his training group. Speaking with the arrogance of youth, he announced: "I *know* I can do a better job for my clients. I've just got to get them to know it, too!"

If enthusiasm made successful advisors, America would be awash with millionaires. But energy and desire, while important, won't accomplish your goal; beating out the incumbent advisor will. To achieve your goal, you must do four things (three of which we've already covered):

- Know What You Don't Know (**Research**)

- Create an Atmosphere for Truth-Telling (**Rapport**)

- Have a Strategy to Find Pain (**Discovery**)

And like the ambitious young advisor above

- Get the Prospect to See How You Can Do a Better Job (**Differentiation**)

There is no step more vital in the sales game than developing a strategy to differentiate yourself from all the other firms and other advisors who are offering nearly identical products and services at nearly identical fees. It is a prime reason why we do research on ourselves and our own firms, and it is the reason why we are focusing on it at length in this chapter.

Let's go back to the "Picture Perfect" wife example I used in Chapter 5. I know it's silly and sexist, but I use it because it illustrates several concepts very effectively, including the value of words that are specific and concrete.

For example, let's try the same conversation this way: "You know, I love being married. My wife is always doing things for me and she really cares about me. Don't you like being married, too?" Same story, but what sort of response will you get this time, strained credulity? No. Chances are the answer would be "Sure! My wife's the same way."

What happened? You just said the same thing, but in a different way. You took a very specific, concrete, image-filled description of an "ideal" (sorry, ladies) wife and reduced it to an abstract generalization. By doing so, you took all the power of differentiation out of your words. Your marriage sounds just like your friend's, so how could he perceive the difference?

Now, let's bring the principle of differentiation back to the real world of sales:

During a sales coaching seminar, one of my favorite exercises as a sales strategist and motivator is to get the participants talking about why their company or firm is better than the competition.

"Firms are as different as night and day," I tell them. "The services, the people, and the way they provide service are vastly different. Please take a moment to list at least four areas where your firm is different or better than your competitors."

The people who attend my workshops are obviously motivated and intelligent, and in a few minutes we have a long list of outstanding features: the latest technology, well-trained employees, commitment to quality service, a solid reputation in the industry, and strong relationships with our clients—the list goes on and on.

Then I present the list their competitors would write and, inevitably, they are identical. Why?

Because as we pointed out earlier, in almost every industry today, the features listed above aren't exceptional, they are the *minimum* standard for doing business. Every company, particularly the major players you're likely to be competing against, are working hard to keep up with new technologies and are using strategies like Team Building to increase productivity and improve customer satisfaction.

Therefore, being different from your competitors is not a function of the differences in the firms themselves, but in the people representing them: the advisors. Your sales style, your ability to cause clients to think critically and perceive a positive difference between your firm and any other, are qualities that are much more vital to success than proving that your firm is "better," based on some arbitrary level of service or the perceived "quality" of your reputation.

> *Remember, among quality, competitive firms, there will be little difference in features or benefits. Listing your firm's features merely meets the "minimum requirements" of doing business and makes you sound like everyone else. The key element is not your product or service: It's YOU!*

So, if you and your competitors are providing essentially the same services, how do you differentiate between you and your competitors?

It's not what you do; it's how you do it: the process by which you provide your service. This is where you can set your firm apart from the competition and create the opportunity for differentiation.

Think of your favorite clothing store. Go to any mall in America, and there are probably dozens of stores that offer the same clothes for about the same price. So what sets your favorite store apart from the rest?

It's the process. It begins when you walk in the door. It's how you're greeted, it's the way the sales clerks size you up, the way they ask you what you are looking for and where you plan to wear it. When you leave the store, you leave with a suit or dress that you could have purchased anywhere. But because of the quality of the process, you chose to buy it from this store and, chances are, you'll be back again. The difference is not in the product, it's in how the product is delivered.

Now think about you and your practice. How do you deliver your product in a way that is different from your competition? We know that the products and services are about the same, so what's different?

Let's return to the example of the clothing store. Every store has clothes, they all have salespeople, they have sales, they take returns—these are the bare bones requirements of being in the clothing business. If this store ran an ad campaign saying "Come to our clothing store! We're different, we have clothes!," you would think that was strange.

But that's precisely how you sound when you sit down with a prospect and start listing the features of your practice, features shared by every firm in the business. Who doesn't claim to offer "quality service?" What company doesn't strive to offer lower risk and higher returns?"

These features are the bare bones of your business. Your job is to put meat on those bones, to flesh out an image of your practice that gives your prospect a detailed and attractive picture of what you can offer. And the bones you want to flesh out are the processes of providing these common services that set you apart.

The first step on your path from selling to winning is to take your focus off of the features of your product or service and to zero-in on the way you and your firm *provide* service, which is the one area where your differences are most likely to stand out.

Sounds simple, right? Unfortunately, simplicity is probably your biggest obstacle.

Climbing Down The Ladder of Abstraction

Think about the words we've been using to describe the characteristics of your firm or practice: quality service, new technology, competitive fees, and customer orientation. All of these words share a characteristic among them-selves. They are abstract.

Abstract concepts like love, hate, humanity, quality, competition, and technology are difficult to visualize. What does "love" look like? Can you draw a picture of "quality?" And if you can't do it, neither can your prospect. If your prospect can't picture what you are offering, he or she will never see the difference between you and the incumbent.

For your prospect to see the differentiation, you must project concrete, easy-to-see images of the service you provide. You do this by climbing down the "ladder of abstraction."

The concept of the "ladder of abstraction" comes from linguist and former US Senator S.I. Hirakata. In his famous book, *Language In Thought and Action*, he puts the language we use on a scale, from abstract to concrete, and uses the ladder as a metaphor to help us choose what level of language we should use.

For example: you are driving to a potential new client meeting and pass a cow standing in a field. When you get to your appointment, you might say: "You know what I saw on the way here? A mammal." Or you could say "I saw Farmer Brown's black cow, Bessie." In both cases, you would be accurate. But the phrase that allows the listener to visualize most precisely what you are describing is "Farmer Brown's black cow, Bessie."

The phrase works because it is concrete, it is at the bottom of the ladder of abstraction. Moving up the ladder, you could say you saw "one of Farmer Brown's cows," "a Hereford," "a cow," "a farm animal," "a mammal," "a quadruped," "a life form," "something."

Each rung of the ladder describes Bessie, just at a different level of abstraction. Your goal when describing how your firm provides its services is to stay as low on the ladder as possible. Telling me you offer "time-sensitive service" does not help me visualize what you will do for me. But letting me know that you guarantee "24-hour turn-around" gives me a clear picture, one that I can compare with the incumbent.

Here's another example:

> It's time for lunch, and you walk down to the corner where there are two restaurants: Abner's Abstract Grill and Cathy's Concrete Cafe. You stick your head in at Abner's and ask "What's good today?" Abner sticks his head out of the kitchen and says "The burgers are very good today. You'll like 'em!"

You walk across the street to Cathy's and ask her the same thing. Cathy says: "I just finished grinding the fresh sirloin for our burgers—it's 98% fat-free and ready to flame-broil on our mesquite grill which is designed to sear in all the juices. We season it with a special blend of Worcestershire, black pepper, and garlic and serve it hot and fresh on a whole wheat sesame seed bun, along with a heaping order of gourmet onion rings."

I ask you, which restaurant makes a better burger? The fact is, Abner's Abstract Grill might prepare his burgers exactly the same way or even better! But because he doesn't relate it in a way that allows you to visualize the qualities of his product, it's just "good." But what does "good" taste like?

If you want your prospect to see the differences between you and your competitors, you must be prepared with well-rehearsed stories and images which avoid abstract phrases that merely meet the minimum standard of service. You want to focus on the way you deliver these services and use concrete images to help your prospect visualize the differences between you and your competitors.

If you use concrete language to help your prospect visualize the way you provide services, you will increase your opportunity to create differentiation and to break apart the incumbent relationship.

Abstract vs. Concrete: The Wedge At Work

Suppose you are an affluent homeowner and you have plans to meet with two insurance agents from different firms.

The agent from firm A sits down and does a few things to establish rapport. Then he starts telling you about his company, its reputation and commitment to quality service. Soon he goes into his presentation about their service standards, number of carriers, and risk management philosophy and asks you for an opportunity to provide a competitive quote and see how they do.

The agent from firm B comes in, and after doing a few things to establish rapport, she begins with a brief story to gain some credibility and then asks a few questions:

Insurance Agent: In a meeting recently with another family, a concern was shared about what might happen in the event of a major storm or household fire. They didn't know for certain that everything would be covered adequately from an insurance perspective. What they said they wanted was to know that everything was properly covered. An analysis was done and now they know. Tell me about your situation.

Prospect: We feel kind of the same way, not exactly sure where we stand with our household insurance.

Insurance Agent: Well, can I ask you this, when your insurance agent comes out to meet with you about 45 days before your renewal to do a coverage review, and they get out a checklist of all of the exposures you and your family have, where one column is checked "yes" if the coverage is in place and one column checked "no" if there is no coverage. They explained what could go wrong and what you could buy to protect it so you wouldn't have to worry about a major claim that you'd have to pay for out of your own pocket. I'm curious if you're comfortable with how they went through that process?

Prospect: They didn't really do that; they just mailed us a questionnaire.

Insurance Agent: And you're OK with that?

Prospect: Not really, it's left us with some uncertainty.

Insurance Agent: Well, let me ask you this. You've got a beautiful home. If something terrible did happen would you want to rebuild it, or would you just move?

Prospect: We love this neighborhood, we'd want to stay here and rebuild.

Insurance Agent: OK. Tell me this. When your agent came out last year at renewal to do a replacement cost analysis, and they noted any and all the special amenities of your home including special trim, wood finish, granite tops, and flooring, then updated your policy with the proper limits so you wouldn't have to worry about getting an inferior finish-out if you had to rebuild it, how did that go?

Remember, selling involves playing the numbers, while winning involves playing the probabilities. Using research to develop strategies for creating rapport, anticipating the prospect's problems, and creating clear, concrete images which highlight your strengths and the incumbent's weaknesses will set up your opportunity to Drive the Wedge.

Forget luck. Luck is for sellers, not winners. There is no substitution for preparation, research, and rehearsal. As a famous golf pro once said, "You know, the harder I work, the luckier I get."

Chapter 7

Picture Perfect

A five-star general is standing in front of a huge picture window in a hospital. He looks out on the idyllic scene before him—a beautiful mountain landscape, blue sky, and evergreen forests—and he thinks to himself, "This is the most perfect scene I could imagine. This is picture perfect."

Why is the person in our little scene a five-star general? Because like generals, prospects want to be in command. They are decision makers and don't like being pushed or pressured. The Wedge acknowledges this and is designed to keep the prospect in command at all times.

Similarly, commanding officers don't like to be told what they've done wrong, and neither do your prospects. The easiest way to get someone to be defensive is to begin attacking the decisions they've made. And yet, for many advisors, this is standard operating procedure. When they see a problem, they go straight at the prospect, with phrases like "Did you know that firm is in the middle of a class action law suit?" or "The Mutual Fund you're in has one of the worst reputations in the industry!"

And what happens? The prospect shuts down. He doesn't want to hear that he's an idiot; that his situation is screwed up, that you're smarter than he is. Would you? Of course not. That's human nature.

The Wedge is a successful strategy for "winning" because it's based *entirely* on human nature. It works because it's easier to get someone to deny things are perfect than it is to admit there's a problem. Picture Perfect is a strategy creating conflict between the prospect and the incumbent by showing the prospect an ideal level of service. As the prospect compares his current level of service to his Picture Perfect vision, the difference he finds is the space into which you drive The Wedge.

You see, perfection is just a standard of service. And it's easier to get someone to say "No, the service I'm getting does not meet *that* standard of excellence" than it is to get someone to say "Yes, I have a problem."

Creating Picture Perfect

The most important word in the concept of Picture Perfect is "picture." The prospect must see, visualize, and have a clear image of the perfect level of service. To create that image, you need concrete words and descriptions that give him something solid to compare against the incumbent.

Giving your prospect the perfect picture requires that you create word pictures, in this case, the picture of ideal service. The key to creating word pictures is to use specific, concrete language, images that are low on the ladder of abstraction.

Think back to our examples in Chapter 5. Remember the guy who said his restaurant has good food. Well, what does "good" look like? What does it smell like?

If you ask the prospect to compare your "good" service, your "customer-oriented approach," and your "commitment to quality" against the incumbent's, you'll lose. You will lose because you're offering the same thing everyone else is. Every business has "good, customer-oriented, quality" service. Every advisor is committed to excellence. Everybody is using the same vague sales talk filled with empty words and no imagery.

This begs the question: Do you have a clear, concrete, and specific image of the service your practice can provide? Can you create a word picture for a prospect that he can mentally hold up next to the incumbent?

If you can't define it, you will never be able to share it with the prospect, he will never be able to use it for comparison. And without that comparison, you look just like the incumbent. You lose.

Nothing is either good or bad except by comparison.

The tough part of selling anything is that to be effective you have to be able to articulate the difference between what you offer the prospect and what the incumbent does. Unless you can create comparisons that show that one option is superior to another, you are just another "seller" wasting a prospect's time. The painful truth is that in most cases your competitors, including the incumbent, probably offer pretty much the same products and services that you do.

So how do you create differences? The winning difference is not in what you do, but rather how you do it. It's in the unique ways that you and your practice deliver products and services that you can create favorable comparisons.

Therefore, the first step towards creating Picture Perfect is to consider what makes you different; the superior ways you provide the services your firm offers. These differences can then be translated directly into benefits to the client.

Then, go through a process like the ones on page 46 in Chapter 5 or on page 55 in Chapter 6, develop a clear, concrete, image-filled description of the ideal level of service. With this description, you create a picture of complete satisfaction and increased benefits for the prospect. When the prospect compares this ideal picture to his or her actual level of current service, the incumbent's performance will be inferior. Dissatisfaction equals pain and pain equals The Wedge.

The Winning Difference

Now let me answer a frequently-asked question: "What if there aren't any major differences between what my firm offers and what my competitors do. In fact, I can't think of any one thing that we do so well that, when I tell the prospect about it, they'll be blown away. Sure, there are some little things I can do that add value—like put together a comprehensive investment plan for them and guarantee same-day responses to questions they have—but there's not one aspect of our service that will just knock their socks off."

And in most cases you're right. The reality is that there are three levels of difference:

1. Something that you do that is absolutely unique.

2.   You have nothing unique, but you have a better method of doing it. For example, anyone can cook a hamburger. It's how you cook it that can make it better, e.g., the right degree of doneness, heat level, seasonings used, and so on.

3.   Your method isn't better than anyone else's. The difference is that you plan ahead and do it without prompting, not just on request.

Let's say that you are in a meeting with an investor and you're doing what a traditional advisor would do. You'd tell them about your firm, how long you've been in business, which money managers you represent, and about your quality service. That's the usual approach. However, since almost every advisor in America does exactly the same thing, the investor is left to make his or her decision on one factor alone: relationship.

So what would a "Wedge" advisor do? By knowing and understanding the "Three Levels of Differentiation" he would do his research and identify the key processes or methods he uses that his competition doesn't that will keep the prospect ahead of the "trouble curve." He would then develop his Proactive Wedge questions before entering the new business sales interview.

Here are some examples of things you might try to differentiate you from the incumbent:

- Investment Plan

- Tax Analysis

- Insurance Review

- Written Services Plan

- Asset Allocation Review

- Risk Management Analysis

The next step in Picture Perfect is to present that perfect picture to the prospect in the right way.

"When You Told Your Advisor That..."

When the average salespeople of the world figure out that they can do something better than the incumbent, the farthest thing from their mind is assuming Picture Perfect. Instead, they inevitably attack their competitor (and, in the process, demean or question the judgment of the prospect). Here's an example:

> **Prospect:** "Our current advisor doesn't seem to be consistent at updating us on a timely basis."
>
> **Advisor:** "You're not being treated fairly. *We* take pride in our ability to serve our customers. We have a monthly newsletter to keep you informed on an ongoing basis. In fact, we have a person in our office dedicated to producing newsletters. And if you'll just call Sally, she'll email them to you. That is what you want isn't it?"

And another prospect shuts down rather than get berated by an advisor.

The Wedge begins not with an attack on the incumbent or a "fishing expedition" of open-ended questions, but by assuming perfection already exists:

> **Prospect:** "Our advisor doesn't seem to be consistent at updating us on a timely basis."
>
> **Advisor:** "I hear that a lot. When you told your current advisor you were unhappy that they didn't update you on a timely basis and that you wanted a call scheduled on a quarterly basis, what did they say?"

Note that there is no challenge to the prospect at all. Questions built on this model assume that the prospect is doing his job; that he has called his (incumbent) advisor and is working on a solution to his problems.

There isn't any challenge to the incumbent either. Once again, you're "assuming" that the incumbent is providing Picture Perfect service. If he isn't, well, that's not your fault.

Why Picture Perfect Works

This approach works because there are three people in on every deal: the prospect, the incumbent and the competitor. And built into every deal are potential points of conflict.

For example, consider the different views these people have on the issue of fees/cost/price. What is the prospect's priority? He wants it as low as possible. What about the incumbent? He wants it to be as high as possible without losing the client.

What about service? The prospect always wants more service and more attention. The incumbent, being human, wants to do as little as possible. In other words, the incumbent wants to do the least amount of work required to keep his client.

This is true in every area of the incumbent's approach, and it might be true in your business life as well. Nobody likes to work any harder than necessary; that's human nature. But because the incumbent is only offering the necessary level of service as opposed to the *ideal* level of service, there is an opportunity to Drive The Wedge.

The Wedge assumes that every party is doing what comes naturally; the prospect wants as much time, service, and attention as he can get, all at the lowest possible cost; and the incumbent wants to spend as little time as possible on his client while collecting as much commission as he can.

More often than not, what comes naturally, "get the most for the least," is the prevailing condition, which is why, more often than not, The Wedge works.

Recap

- The easiest way to get someone to be defensive is to begin attacking the decisions they have made.

- It is easier to get someone to deny things are perfect than it is to admit there is a problem

- Nothing is either good or bad except by comparison.

Chapter 8

The Take Away

The story thus far:

- You have shown the prospect the picture perfect level of service and performance.

- You have found the pain, the problem or challenge that the prospect believes is truly important and feels strongly about addressing.

Your prospect has seen Picture Perfect: the level of service that he can imagine, but does not have. His reaction is clear: he's not satisfied with the service he's getting.

The question now is: How much does he care? Is he truly feeling "pain?" Is he ready to make a change?

To find out, we are going to show him another picture, the flip side of Picture Perfect: the Take Away. By dismissing the prospect's pain and "taking away" the benefits he would achieve by solving his problem, you will help the prospect see clearly what will be lost if he fails to act.

How The Take Away Works

As a process, the "Take Away" is very simple: You clearly state the price of inaction and then dismiss it. As a technique, the "Take Away" is extremely effective.

Let's say the prospect has told you that the incumbent advisor is not doing the job, that there is distance between the service he is receiving and the service which is available. The prospect has either volunteered this information (a Reactive Wedge) or you have helped him discover it by using the Picture Perfect technique (a Proactive Wedge).

At this point, if the incumbent advisor were in the room, he would lunge right at the prospect with a pitch: "Boy, you must really be upset that you aren't getting the turn-around time you need. This must really be tough for you. If you were my client, I can assure you we would do a great job. Are you ready to get started?"

To which the answer is likely to be, "Naw, it's not that big a deal. We've got it under control. It's no big deal, really." You've just "sold" yourself out of a deal.

The Wedge is not about "selling" anything. The Wedge works because it helps the prospect go through a process of self-discovery. When you sat down with the prospect, he didn't know he was unhappy with his current level of service because he didn't have a true vision of how these services or products could be better. Using the Picture Perfect technique, he has discovered that he has a problem where he had not seen one before. It was always there. You didn't create it. You just helped him discover it.

The next step, the Take Away, allows the prospect to discover how important solving this problem truly is, how much it matters. For example, you are talking with the head of a household that has been gathering assets at a significant rate for the past several years, and you ask him this question:

Advisor: "When your advisor came out at the last quarterly review to rebalance your portfolio, he got out your financial plan with the recommended asset allocation, along with your account summary which showed your current allocation, and compared them to determine where you're out of balance. He then made adjustments in your portfolio so that you wouldn't have to worry about taking too much risk and losing value, or too little risk and losing return. I'm curious, were you comfortable with how they went through the process?"

Prospect: "He never came out to do that."

Advisor: "And that's not that important!"

If this is a typical person, he won't like those kinds of surprises. He won't enjoy risk either. Most likely he'll respond with something like, "Hell yeah, that's a big deal."

If you had warned him that these kinds of surprises could bring on a disastrous situation that could put his financial strength at risk, he would have dismissed it as "selling." And he would be right. But by dismissing it for him, you force the prospect to think about how important this problem truly is. He has to commit, intellectually, to the importance of solving the problem at hand.

There are a million Take Aways, one for every benefit you and your product or service can provide. However, the format is almost always the same.

You always begin with the Wedge subject, the specific improvement in products or services that you have presented to the prospect. You then dismiss it as unimportant, as "no big deal," or "not a significant problem.

If your Take Away is accurate, and the issue is not particularly important to the prospect, he will let it go by. By doing so, the prospect is letting you know that you need to move on to another Wedge issue and another concern.

But if you have found true pain in the prospect, if you have raised an issue that would be important enough to consider firing the incumbent over, the prospect will not allow it to be dismissed. Instead of resisting your suggestions of a need to change, he will assert his own belief that change may be in order.

Why The Take Away Works

The Take Away is based on a rather primitive notion called the Boy/Girl Theory, which says that what you have you don't want, and what you haven't got, you're always lusting after. Not sophisticated, perhaps, but true.

The lesson of Boy/Girl theory is not that you should "play hard to get," but that pushing someone to do something almost always creates resistance, no matter how beneficial the action you are pushing may be. Prospects are people; they aren't computers. If they feel put off, if they sense that they are being pressured, the emotional response is enough to kill the deal.

The Take Away is a 180-degree approach. Instead of pushing someone to agree with you that it's time to make a change, you push them to defend the benefits of change. When you say "You absolutely must...," the natural human reaction is to be contrary and say "No, I don't."

But when you say "Don't bother doing..., it's not that important," the natural human reaction is to say "Now wait a minute. Doing might be the best thing for me and my family. Let's talk about it."

If this all seems like a game, you might be right. But the game only works when the prospect is truly moving forward in the process of self-discovery.

The Take Away technique is vital if your prospect is going to discover the need for change. Every day, prospects "intellectualize" problems and challenges their families face that they either cannot or do not solve. Remember, if you "sell" the need for change, the customer is almost always willing to resist, to say it's no big deal, and continue to deny the legitimate needs you have identified.

So they don't re-balance their portfolio, one day, what happens? They get "stung."

But when they do get stung, whose fault is it? The Incumbent's, the Prospect's, or Yours? Did you do your job if you let them "off the emotional hook" because you started selling, convincing, or persuading? If you did, the prospect missed the opportunity to better themselves by working with you and will eventually pay the price.

Here's an example that is close to home for most of us. Most of us have families. We have spouses and children who depend on us. We know that we should be preparing for the future, we know that Social Security won't pro-vide all of the financial support we are going to need when we get older. But we justify our failure to act by pushing back that timeline, by rationalizing our failure to save, invest, or prepare for the inevitable. Deep down inside, in our latent memories, we know we need to act. But we justify our inaction and ignore our problem.

Then a salesman knocks on our door and points out that legitimate need. And what do we do? We convince this so-called "high pressure salesman" that we will figure it out one day, so we don't need his insurance policy, investment product, or savings plan. And you know what? That salesperson is a failure. He didn't fail because he didn't make a sale. He failed because he let us down. We needed to act, and he didn't do his job and create within us the stimulus to do so.

I know this first hand. My father died in 1998. And somewhere out there, there is a financial advisor who let him off the hook. My dad could have made payments on a life insurance policy, he could have started an investment program, and he could have put a plan in action.

If the financial advisor had done what was best for my dad instead of what was easier for him, my dad would have implemented a financial plan. And it would have been the best thing for him.

But he didn't. My father didn't see clearly the benefits of acting or the costs of inaction; all he could see was the few extra dollars each month in premiums and savings. And my mom is paying the price today.

Whose fault is it? Of course, my father had to take responsibility. However, the person I blame is that financial advisor out there who didn't get my father to see the vision he needed to.

The Challenge of the "Take Away"

In my years of sales training, I have found that the Take Away is one of the most difficult concepts for people to master. Why?

Part of the reason is that the Take Away is so counter-intuitive. In the Take Away, you are generally saying the opposite of what you really mean. Your words may be saying "Oh, it's no big deal…," but your tone and demeanor are screaming: "What are you, crazy? You've got to do something about this problem!"

As such, "Take Aways" are incongruent messages, and the tension gets people's attention. Psychologically, they throw people off balance. It takes a little getting used to, but it is a powerful and effective technique.

Another reason advisors tend to have problems with the Take Away is because many people don't want the responsibility that comes from truly being able to make a difference in the lives of others.

For an advisor who claims to believe in the products and services he sells and the company he represents, The Wedge can be very dangerous. Because if the things you are telling your prospects are true, then you have a duty to help them discover the benefit that is available to them and to help them take action now.

The advisors I work with have realized: "Hey, if I see the legitimate problems the prospect is facing, but I can't find a way to get him to see them too, then it is my fault." If you fail to get them to discover and own their problems, you aren't just letting yourself and your firm down, but you're also letting the prospect down.

It doesn't matter what you sell or how tangible or intangible the product or service may be. If you can provide your products or services in a way that will honestly benefit your clients, it's your responsibility to find a way to get them to see it.

Recap

- If you fail to get the prospect to discover and own his problem, you aren't just letting yourself and your firm down; you're letting the prospect down.

Chapter 9

Vision Box
and Replay

U p to this point:

- You have shown the prospect the "Picture Perfect" level of service and performance.

- You have found the pain, the problem or challenge that the prospect believes is truly important and feels strongly about addressing.

- Using the "Take Away," you have helped the prospect articulate clearly that solving this problem is important to him, committing himself emotionally and intellectually to a solution.

For some of the more entrenched advisors, the "Vision Box" is the most difficult technique to master because it requires the advisor to do something completely out of character: *Let someone else talk.*

But for those advisors well-schooled in the "open-ended question" approach, the "Vision Box" will be your opportunity to shine. You will need your questioning skills too, because this isn't a "bull" session we're talking about. As in every step of The Wedge, you have a very specific task in mind.

The task is to get a "Vision Box" statement from the prospect that is as clear, concrete, and visual as the Picture Perfect you gave him earlier. If you can do that you will have achieved your goal. But it won't be easy.

"The Vision Box at Work"

Thanks to the "Take Away," the prospect has made the emotional commitment to change. He has "seen" the level of service he wants and has said that achieving it is important. But so far, you've done most of the talking. The prospect has seen *your* vision of the future. Now it's time for you to see his.

If you used the rapport techniques discussed earlier and created an environment of comfort and credibility, then getting the prospect to talk will not be a problem. Getting him to tell you what he wants, that's the problem.

You see, prospects have the same problems communicating that advisors do. They want to "provide for their family," they're interested in a "secure future," and they have "long-term goals."

The prospect has seen the benefits of change. He honestly believes you can help him get where he wants to go, only he can't tell you where that is. Like the sales people from Chapter Five who were stuck way up on the ladder of abstraction, the prospect will tell you he wants to go "North," when he really wants to go to the corner of Main and Elm in downtown Milwaukee, Wisconsin.

So the challenge is to ask questions that will encourage the prospect to fill out the "Vision Box"—in your mind and in his—with a clear, colorful, concrete image of the services he wants, the problems he would like to solve, and the new way he would like to do business.

How do you do this? By using outstanding communication skills, along with intelligent, planned, and well-rehearsed questioning to help the prospect fill in the concrete details of abstract concepts like 1) "Construct a portfolio" or 2) "Provide for family" or 3) "Finally get consistent and significant savings over the long-term."

"So, What Would You Like To Have Happen?"

The first essential question will be, "How would you like this [the specific area of the prospect's need where you have found the pain] to work? What would you like to see happen?" This question is likely to elicit a vague answer, no matter how specifically you ask, so use follow-up questions to help the prospect define his terms, set specific goals, and detail the solutions to problems of the past which have left him dissatisfied.

The key thing to remember about the "Vision Box" is that you can be almost certain that the prospect doesn't know what he wants to begin with. He may know he's dissatisfied, and he may want "better service" or "more hands-on support," but those comments are so high up the infamous "ladder of abstraction" that they are essentially useless.

The advisor's job at this point is to help the prospect "down the ladder" until the description of his vision of ideal service is so clear that you can repeat it back to him. Intelligent, directed questioning can help.

Pertinent questions include: When you say "_____," what do you mean? You've mentioned growth: do you have specific goals? When you say you want "_____," how would that work? What, specifically, would you like to change?

The key is to elicit specifics, i.e., concrete language and images. If the prospect says "I would like to get my reports faster," your question should be: "How fast? What do you really need?" If he says he wants regular meetings with the advisor, find out if regular means once a quarter or once a year!

This process is called the Vision Box for a reason. Until the prospect has a clear, concrete, descriptive vision of what he actually wants, you won't know what he wants from you. Remember, chances are the incumbent offers the same products and services you do. He just hasn't taken advantage of the opportunity to find out what is truly important to the client, how he can truly help the client succeed and how the client wants them packaged.

When you have a clear vision of the client's goals and aspirations, and a real, workable approach to help him achieve these goals—when you have all this and the incumbent doesn't—you've made progress, but you haven't won yet.

The Replay

The next step is to make sure that you understand the client's desires and objectives by repeating them back to him; be clear and specific. This is "The Replay."

There isn't much more to be said about The Replay other than one final, very important point that applies to both The Replay and The Vision Box. During these two steps, your greatest temptation and worst enemy will be to use the words "me" and "I." *Avoid them at all costs.*

During the Vision Box and Replay parts of a prospect meeting, I like to think of myself as an "architect" who has a friend planning to build a house. Because he is a friend, and I'm in the building business, I'm interested in his plans and excited about seeing his vision fulfilled. I'm not, however, trying to sell my services as "the contractor."

We talk about windows, landscaping, the latest household gadgets, and building techniques as my friend tries to get me to envision his dream house; and I try to ask specific questions that make that vision clearer for both of us.

As long as we're talking about how my friend wants to get "somebody" in to put down a masonry floor or custom design a walk-in closet, the conversation is both honest and enthusiastic.

But what happens as soon as I say, "Buddy, let me build this house for you. I'll give you a good price." Suddenly, we're negotiating instead of communicating. He stops telling me what he really wants and starts telling me what he thinks he can afford. I become a seller, and he becomes a buyer.

Somehow, we want the conversation to transition naturally from the prospect talking about "somebody" to the prospect asking "how can *you* help me?" You want this to happen because the prospect has asked, not because you have suggested it.

The temptation is to say "Let me do this" or "Our firm offers everything you need." Don't do it. Don't start selling because, as soon as you start with "I can do this," or "Let me take care of…," the prospect feels it and begins shutting down. He starts thinking: "If I'm not careful, somebody is going to be asking me for a check. I'd better shut up."

Don't tell, ask; don't talk, listen. Once you have the clear vision, lay it out so that he can see you have it, and will conclude you can help him achieve it.

You want to help the prospect create a mental bridge between points A and B, with the "building materials" provided by you. When the prospect sees you as the bridge between where he is and the benefits of where he could be, he will ask you. And when you're being asked, you have all the power.

Chapter 10

The White Flag

T he story so far:

- You have shown the prospect the Picture Perfect level of service and performance.

- You have found the pain, the problem or challenge that the prospect believes is truly important and feels strongly about addressing.

- Using the Take Away, you have helped the prospect clearly articulate that solving this problem is important to him, committing emotionally and intellectually to a solution.

- You heard the prospect's vision of the level of service he would like to receive, and you gave him a Replay of that vision by going back over it with him.

If you've successfully followed the first five steps of the Wedge, and you get to the final step—"The White Flag"—the prospect will appear so ready to buy that every fiber in your body will be tingling with the desire to "Sell, Sell, Sell!" Don't do it.

Remember, you aren't in the "selling" business anymore. The Wedge gets you out of the selling business and into the closing business, the "winning" business. The average salesperson wants to go on the attack, throwing sales babble at the prospect and sticking contracts under people's noses. That's selling, and it doesn't work.

I know what you're thinking: "Randy, you're out of your mind! I've got this guy! He's beggin' me to sell. I can feel it! Let me sell!"

That's the temptation. The Wedge has helped the prospect discover for himself that he wants and needs to make a change, and you want to pitch yourself and your firm as the solution. It makes sense. It's exactly what a seller would do—ask the prospect to buy.

But winners know that the strongest position to be in is for the prospect to *buy—asking you to please do it!*

Advisors spend their time asking prospects to buy…and being rejected. When you are out pushing yourself and your product, everything is working against you. You are on the wrong side of the Boy/Girl Theory. The laws of physics, particularly inertia, are aligned against you. Not surprisingly, when you "sell," you don't often close. Using The Wedge means taking the opposite approach so, when done properly, instead of pushing the prospect to buy, you're pushed by the prospect to sell (Buyer's Facilitation Process).

In the last chapter, we used the example of an architect listening to a friend's plans to build a house. Let's return to that for a minute. If the architect has been a true friend, helping his pal visualize the picture perfect home and showing him how to achieve it, the perfectly natural conclusion of that conversation is for the architect's friend to ask him: "Can you help me build this dream house?"

At the same time, it would be very unnatural, and rather annoying, for the architect to ask his friend for a check. Friends don't ask friends to submit bids.

If you can create the natural dynamic between you and the prospect of two friends working together to achieve a goal, you have created the best possible opportunity to win (CBO & SRU). Everything that was working against the seller is working for you as the friend being asked to step in and help.

Falling On The Sword

The sixth and final step is not for you to assault the prospect's "fortress," but for the prospect to lower the drawbridge and invite you in. The example I use to illustrate this is "The Sword."

For too many advisors, selling is a sword that they wield, slashing and attacking others, spreading fear and dread wherever they go. They see their sales pitch as a weapon they use to force reluctant prospects to capitulate. These people don't want to join the prospect's team, they want the would-be customer to yield before their superior sales firepower.

You can see it in their presentations: They line up their statistics like cannons on a ridge. They "target" the return's/yield's weaknesses ("I can beat the return he's getting" or "I'm gonna stomp all over his current investment selection"). They prepare for battle, put on their lucky three-piece suit and, at the first sign of prospect pain, they unsheathe their sales "sword" and start slashing away! Not surprisingly, these advisors are rarely greeted with open arms by their prospects.

If you must view your services and benefits as a sword, that's OK. However, we don't want to use the sword to "defeat" the prospect/incumbent relationship by force. We want the prospect to pick up the sword himself and sever his ties to the incumbent.

For the prospect, it's the difference between being attacked and overcome by the advisor—never a pleasant experience—and realizing for himself that he needs to make a change, and then willingly choosing to do so.

How The White Flag Works

The prospect is sitting across from you, convinced that it's time for a change, that there is both a problem and, he hopes, a solution. But he has yet to take a single action committing himself to that change.

At this point in the process, the primary obstacle to closing isn't the prospect. It's you and your desire to rush forward and seize the deal for yourself. "Let me tell you how my firm can make the changes you need" is a sentence that resides on the tip of every seller's tongue.

But you aren't going to do that. Instead, you are going to conclude the Replay of the prospect's vision of how he would like his problems solved by asking the question: "So, what would you like me to do?" The prospect isn't under assault. He is in control.

If you have established rapport and helped the prospect discover the kind of true pain that can drive The Wedge deeply, his response to your question will be to invite you in immediately.

Ideally, the prospect will affirmatively indicate that he is prepared to act. You will hear statements that begin with questions like "Can you really help me…" or "I'm ready to go" or "Will you put together a summary or proposal?"

And, of course, you will oblige. But before you tell him that, you need to resume the prospect's journey of self-discovery because the second obstacle that might prevent him from buying is his inability to see that his problem is the incumbent.

Your job is to get the prospect to see that the specific business problems facing him (the pain that has driven the Wedge) are just symptoms. The prospect must see that the only way to cure these symptoms—higher costs, slow turn-around time, ongoing technical problems—is to deal with the real problem, the incumbent advisor or practice. *They* are the reason why the prospect is dissatisfied and he must see that clearly before he will be ready to act.

By saying to you "Can you lower my costs" or "can you put an end to all the technical glitches," the prospect is saying, in effect, anyone who can solve these problems is the solution—including the incumbent. And, of course, if the incumbent gets the chance, he will promise to make everything right too. Most likely he will try to use his relationship with the prospect to keep you blocked out.

So, when the prospect asks for your help, the answer isn't "Sure! Let me bring in a proposal next week!" If you give him that answer, he will spend the week being sweet-talked by the incumbent. And why not? After all, the prospect figures that the (incumbent) advisor isn't the problem, the unsatisfactory service is.

If you don't leave the prospect with the belief that the unsatisfactory service is a result of inattentiveness and inability, you've failed. Because soon after you leave with an opportunity to propose in your pocket, the prospect's old pal the incumbent is going to show up with a bottle of scotch and a couple of glasses. He's going to sit down across from your prospect and remind him about the lunches they've shared and the gifts they exchanged during the holidays. He's going to confess to his failings, promise to fix every problem you've identified, and make your prospect's dream come true. If necessary, he'll tell the client in a quivering voice about lil' "Incumbent Jr." who's in college and how much his Daddy needs this account to pay the tuition.

In short, the incumbent is going to make it as hard as possible for the prospect to make a change. Change is painful, and, if the incumbent has anything to say about it, it will be more painful to change than to do nothing, even if the service isn't all it could be.

Suddenly you've gone from a prospect who is practically begging to buy, to a prospect who won't take your calls. Congratulations! You've just been "rolled."

The prospect must see that the incumbent is the problem, that what he is asking you to do is to help him fire the incumbent, not just fix the symptoms. He needs to see precisely what is involved in making the change from the incumbent to you. To do this, we use the "Rehearsal" technique.

Here's the Rehearsal at work:

Prospect: "I'd like you to give me a proposal on how you can help me achieve these goals."

Advisor: "OK. I'd be happy to, in fact, that's the easy part. Can we talk about the hard part?"

Prospect: "What do you mean?"

Advisor: "Suppose for a moment that it's three weeks from now, you're looking at my proposal, and it has everything you've asked for. The three key elements we just went over are all in there and you are confident that it will make a difference for you and your family. Can you imagine that?"

Prospect: "OK. I can imagine that."

Advisor: "As you look at the proposal and say to yourself 'I think I've found a new advisor,' that creates a dilemma. I'm wondering, can we deal with that?"

Prospect: "What's the dilemma?"

Advisor: "The problem is when you decide that you want to make this change, how are you going to tell your current advisor that it's over?"

Prospect: "Hmmm, I never thought about it...."

And now, ladies and gentlemen, we are at the crux of the matter. Recall the first page of this book. Why do we need The Wedge? Because until the prospect is ready to fire, dismiss, lay-off, pink slip, get rid of, or say goodbye to the incumbent, you don't have a real prospect! You can frame it any way you want, but until the incumbent is gone you can't get in!

The Rehearsal is the moment that the prospect realizes this and prepares, in his mind, to fire the incumbent. If he will not fire the incumbent, you will not win. Our entire strategy is to get the prospect to see the benefits of change, to feel the need for change, to have a clear, concrete vision of a brighter future. But it will not work if the prospect can't go through the pragmatic steps of actually making the change, which means firing the incumbent.

The Rehearsal technique takes the prospect into that future moment when he is going to fire the incumbent, show the prospect how difficult it is going to be, and take him through a rehearsal of how to get it done.

Let's return to our dialog:

Prospect: "Hmmm, I never thought about it...."

Advisor: "Well, can I tell you what's going to happen when your advisor finds out you are making a change? He'll want to meet with you...."

At this point you'll coach your client through how to effectively deal with what the incumbent will say when they know they are about to lose the business. Remember, if your prospect can't fire, dismiss, lay off, pink slip, get rid of, or say goodbye to the incumbent, you don't have a prospect!

Why "Rehearse"?

When dealing with a prospect involved in an unsatisfactory incumbent relationship, you face an interesting dilemma: The prospect's heart and mind are in the "wrong place."

If the prospect is unsatisfied with the service he's getting from the incumbent, why hasn't he made a change? Because he is "rationalizing" his pain. He has either decided that there is no such thing as perfect service and that this is the best he can get, that his problem isn't important enough to worry about, or he has pushed it out of his mind and intends to deal with it later. His pain is real, but he has rationalized his way out of dealing with it.

Meanwhile, he is rationalizing his legitimate disappointment or concern and has "emotionalized" the relationship he has with the incumbent. He doesn't want his advisor, who he knows, to feel bad. "Hey, nobody's perfect" is the defense mechanism of a customer who knows that he's not totally satisfied with his advisor's performance but doesn't want the emotional stress of making a change.

The Rehearsal technique is a valuable way to deal with this problem. It works by walking the prospect through the emotional experience of an unpleasant task—firing someone—so that he or she can deal with it on a purely intellectual level when the time comes.

Therapists often use this technique. They use it to prepare people in counseling for a future event, removing the emotional edge of their client's likely response and helping them react intellectually. They will tell clients things like "When you go home, your husband is going to…. How will you react? How do you want to react?"

These questions don't displace or deny emotions. Instead, they bring the emotions out, allowing for a release. When the counselor says "Your husband is going to tell you…," the subject feels the emotions rising and can deal with them in a "Rehearsal" setting. Nothing's on the line, and there is a very friendly audience.

If this seems a little too much like social work, think about how often you see these situations every day. You're in the office and you see a fellow employee is really annoyed about something. You walk into her office and say, "Hey, how's it going?" She unloads on you about how the manager took away a project or didn't give her the schedule she had been promised. The point is, when she is done with the legitimate emotional reaction (i.e. "venting"), she is in a much better frame of mind to confront the manager and deal with the issues at hand.

By talking through the problem with you, and letting off emotional steam, she is now ready to take care of the matter in a more thoughtful, controlled way. But until she resolved the emotional conflict, she was not prepared.

Your prospects are the same way. If the issue were just "do you like me, the salesman, and want to hire me?", we would all be closing 90% of the time. But there is an incumbent out there, and we can't acquire the new client until both the prospect and the incumbent have dealt with the oncoming change.

Chapter 11

Finding Your Winning Wedge Every Time

The Story thus far:

1. You have shown the prospect the **Picture Perfect** level of service and performance.

2. You have found the pain, the problem or challenge that the prospect believes is truly important and feels strongly about addressing.

3. Using the **Take Away**, you have helped the prospect articulate clearly that solving this problem is important to him, committing himself emotionally and intellectually to a solution.

4. You have heard the prospect's **Vision** of the level of service he would like to receive, and you gave him a **Replay** of that vision by going back over it with him.

5. Because you "surrendered with the **White Flag** "instead of selling, the prospect has invited you in, literally asking you to sell to him.

6. You point out that selling to him will create a dilemma: What about the incumbent? Using the **Rehearsal** technique, you help the prospect realize that, to achieve his goals, the prospect must fire the incumbent.

You acquire the client…and **Win!**

These are the six steps of The Wedge and, if I were a typical salesperson, I would tell you that "They are guaranteed to work…every time!" But the entire philosophy of The Wedge is to develop an honest strategy to deal with the real problems preventing you from winning, and I'm not going to start lying to you now.

So let me tell you right now: The Wedge doesn't *always* work.

Sometimes you'll know five minutes into the meeting that no matter what you do, this prospect will find a way to kill the deal. Other times, you won't be able to find any pain. The prospect is going to beam with satisfaction at his incumbent's service. Then there will always be those people who just don't believe anything an advisor says, who won't see a dime's worth of difference between you and every other advisor in the world, no matter what you say or do.

That's reality. But while The Wedge doesn't guarantee success, it does drastically increase your odds by giving you a winning strategy before you even begin your meeting. The six steps of The Wedge that we've covered will have an immediate impact on your business. You will acquire more clients and assets; you will win more.

Of course there's no such thing as a sure thing and you are going to run into situations like the ones mentioned below. Don't panic. There are some additional strategies that you can use to increase your chances to close these deals, too.

Broken Deal #1:
The Prospect Isn't Convinced You Can Get The Job Done

You've gotten the prospect to talk about the pain he's having with the incumbent's service. He's told you his Vision for the level of service he would like to have and you've done a Replay showing that you understand clearly. But when you ask, "OK, what would you like me to do?", his answer is "Well, what *can* you do?"

The prospect knows he could use some help. He's just not convinced that you can help him. And, quite frankly, why should he be?

We live in an era of heightened cynicism. Your prospects have sales hacks barging through their door every day, making promises and throwing around charts, graphs, and guarantees. If the prospect is a good businessperson, he already knows the service he's receiving isn't the best. He has probably tried to solve the problem once or twice already. He may have concluded that what he's got is the industry standard, that satisfactory service just isn't available.

What you need for Doubting Thomases like this is a plan to help them convince themselves that you and your firm can deliver. No, that doesn't mean "selling" with a new set of handouts and five more pages of statistics. That's not strategy, that's just a heavier dose of the same old snake oil.

The "Convincer Strategy" works because it acknowledges that you can't actually "convince" anyone of anything. People must discover the truth for themselves.

There are five basic ways people get information to convince themselves that something is true: their own senses of sight, hearing, touch, taste, and smell. Set aside the last two and we can build a strategy that allows doubting prospects to see, hear, or feel what they must to convince themselves they can move forward with you.

When the prospect's doubt appears, you want to offer a solution that will meet his or her criteria for certainty. When the prospect says, "Can you help me?," you want to let him know that you are aware of the problem. Here's an example:

Advisor: "So, what would you like me to do?"

Prospect: "I don't know. What *can* you do?"

Advisor: "We can fix this problem. I feel we're the best at it…but you expect me to say that, don't you?"

Prospect: "Sure, I guess."

Advisor: "So how would you know that when I tell you we can get it done that I'm telling you the truth? Do you need to see a plan of action? Do you need to see letters of reference? Do you want to talk to some people I've worked with and let them tell you themselves? Or do you go with your gut feeling? How would *you* know?"

You have just offered the prospect a menu of Convincer options from which he can choose. You give him the opportunity to come back in one of those primary modes. And, because you are working the Wedge, you have a strategy for each answer.

For example, if he says he wants to see the plan—"I gotta see the numbers for myself before I can make a decision"—here is your response:

> **Advisor:** "Let's say I come back with three or four letters from people that say we do a great job, along with a written plan that solves this problem. What happens next?"

> **Prospect:** "You do that, and I'll seriously consider making a change."

> **Advisor:** "When you do, that is going to create a new dilemma. I wonder if we can talk about that…."

You are now in the Rehearsal technique outlined in the previous chapter. The same technique works if the prospect wants to talk to your references:

> **Advisor:** "You say you like to talk to people. How many people would you like to talk to?"

> **Prospect:** "Oh, two or three. Maybe four."

> **Advisor:** "If I give you those names, will you call them?"

> **Prospect:** "Sure."

> **Advisor:** "Can I count on that?"

> **Prospect:** "Yes, you can."

> **Advisor:** "OK. Let's suppose you speak to them and they tell you that we are for real, that we can do what we say we can do. What happens next?"

Prospect: "If they do that, I'll be ready to make a switch."

Advisor: "And that's going to create a dilemma for you...."

And we're back in the "Rehearsal."

If they're like a lot of the old-style businesspeople who work off of instinct, there isn't as much room for strategy. If I have a prospect who is clearly dubious about my ability to deliver what we both know he wants, and they tell me they are the "go with the gut" type, I usually just ask, "Well, how am I doing?"

In a surprising number of instances, that question alone resolves the doubt. I usually get a response like "You're doin' fine" or "I'm with you" something along those lines. By asking the question, you will demonstrate that you are listening, that you understand the problem and the need to solve it.

The Convincer strategy is a proven, workable technique that can turn an entire deal around. It works on the premise that the customer cares more about his finances than you do (a realistic assumption) and wants it to grow and prosper. He wants solutions. It also acknowledges all of the damage that has been done to business relationships by "sellers."

Broken Deal #2:
The Shallow Wedge

Sometimes, even the most experienced advisors just can't find any pain. You may have identified a problem the prospect would like to solve, but not one that he perceives as important enough to justify the pain of making a change. Without the emotional force of true pain, the Wedge has "glanced off," and you are not in a position to close.

What do you do? Go back and look again. Use a Proactive Wedge to raise an issue you haven't discussed before. If that doesn't work, use another. As long as the rapport is there and you have Proactive Wedges to drive, keep going. If there was enough discontent there to keep you moving forward the first time, chances are the pain exists. You just need to keep looking for its true source.

This is why it's important to always have several Proactive Wedges prepared before you go into any prospect meeting. Sellers have to rely on their one pitch and hope it works. Not you. You've prepared, you've rehearsed, and you are going to create opportunity after opportunity to have a legitimate shot at winning.

Broken Deal #3:
The Bad Feeling

The one thing that I hope this book has proven to you beyond any doubt is that most of our success is driven by emotion. If you connect with a prospect, if you can establish rapport, if you can help him see the possibility of achieving what he hopes to achieve, you can establish a powerful emotional bond in a matter of minutes.

At the same time, it is possible to have the opposite reaction with a prospect. He looks at you, and you look at him, and wham! Loathing at first sight. Modeling and mirroring won't help. The chemistry is wrong, and nothing will go right.

What do you do?

If you feel it, say it. If you feel that the meeting just isn't working, let the prospect know that you know it, too. The worst thing that can happen is that you save yourself and the prospect a few wasted minutes. And it's always possible that acknowledging an awkward situation will break the ice and give you another opportunity to connect.

You just look at the prospect and say, "I sense that this is not working. Is that a fair statement?" It's a gutsy strategy, to be sure, but once again, we're trying to create a climate for truth-telling. Being that direct has the potential to create deal-breaking levels of confrontation, but dishonesty isn't going to create opportunity, anyway.

"Up or Out" should be your approach. Either you and your prospect are going to move upward toward mutual understanding and communication, or you should get out of his office and go to another appointment.

Summary

This chapter could be an entire book in itself, because the number of things that can go wrong in a prospect meeting are as varied and unpredictable as the prospects themselves. The prospects aren't going to quote directly out of these sample scripts anymore than you are.

However, the principles are always the same. The prospect's concerns and motivations will be the same. And you will be prepared to address every obstacle, dodge every strategy of the prospect's game—no matter how unexpected or unusual—if you will commit yourself to this approach:

- Know what your prospect's concerns and problems are likely to be, so you can anticipate them.

- Establish rapport, so that you can help your prospect on his journey of self-discovery regarding his business and his relationship with the incumbent.

- Identify pain, which is the source of the energy you need, to break the incumbent relationship.

- Concretely demonstrate how you and your firm can deliver the goods and services the prospect needs in a way that will resolve that pain and satisfy his goals for his company.

- Tell the truth.

- Connect personally with the prospect.

- Paint perfect pictures of service for the prospect to compare with the incumbent's real level of service.

- Never offer to act, always position yourself to be invited to ask.

- Force the prospect to clearly state what he truly wants to accomplish.

- Repeat your understanding of the prospect's desires back to him, and listen carefully to his response.

- Never forget that the prospect's problem is not the unsatisfactory product or service, it is the incumbent advisor who is providing that product or service.

- Never forget your Number One obstacle in every deal is the incumbent.

Master these techniques, learn these principles, and you will be able to enter every meeting with a prospective client knowing that you will have a legitimate opportunity to win. More importantly, you will leave every meeting knowing that you explored every opportunity to put yourself in a winning position, no matter what the result.

When you can conclude every business day with these confidences, you'll no longer be selling, *you'll be winning.*

Chapter 12

How to Become a Million Dollar Advisor

One thing that should become clear from this book is the critical importance of having a strong proactive services platform. My mantra, the mantra we all should be chanting, is this: *"Your job as an advisor is to proactively control the experiences of your clients and make their future more predictable."* Your ability to powerfully differentiate your proactive services in a way that removes your prospect's "pain" is the indispensable key to making The Wedge work with maximum effect.

When you start to build and develop your product and services platform, in Financial Services or any other industry, you look at three components: (1) price, (2) product, and (3) service. When it comes to price, the problem we all run into is that there's little difference among the players. The last person in with a good price, usually the incumbent, wins. Similarly, there is no significant variation among advisors in the products they offer at given prices. So it's impossible to create significant competitive advantage here. Moreover, many advisors sell on their ability to react to clients' needs or *reactive* service. They say: We're here for you. They respond well when called upon, but so does everybody else.

Therefore, your strongest differentiation, your greatest competitive advantage, lies in *proactive* service. If you drill down and define in concrete terms the things that you do without prompting that make your client's life easier, and then put those things in a written services timeline that makes renewal a non-issue, you can begin taking full advantage of the power of The Wedge to bust incumbent relationships and seriously grow your book of business (GDC).

Million Dollar Advisors – How to Double Your GDC in Three Years with Half the Clients.

How can you become a Million Dollar Advisor? The formula is simple, Double your GDC in three years with half as many clients. You could try to do it with twice as many clients, but the problem is that you simply run out of time.

According to research done by my good friend Travis Chaney of Dynamic Directions, the hourly rate for an advisor serving the Top 20% of clients was $756 per hour. The hourly rate for service to the Bottom 40% of clients was $65. Do your own math, and see where your numbers come out.

So what's the secret? There isn't one, it's a simple 4 step process of Position, Leverage, Growth, and Scoreboard.

First, you *position* your client base for profitability and growth by over-serving the top 20% of your clients who account for 80% of your revenue, putting them on a written services timeline that makes retention a non-issue. Then you work hard to more deeply penetrate your middle 40% to manage all the assets, and you consider dropping your unprofitable or marginal bottom 40% altogether.

By over-serving your top 20% in this manner, you earn the right to *leverage* them to get introduced to people they know that are your ideal prospects. By working this systematically, what are the chances that in the next 36 months you could get personal introductions from each of your top 20% of clients to another client of equal size, and write it? If you could, you're well on your way to achieving $2n^{3/2}$.

Next, you accelerate your *growth* by using The Wedge to bust incumbent relationships. You've learned how to do that by reading this book.

Finally, you track your growth on a *scoreboard* where you follow such performance indicators as average revenue per client and closing ratios.

If you're an advisor and you are committed to achieving $2n^{3/2}$, there are five areas where you should be spending 80% of your time. I call these the Five Money-Making Activities of Advisors, and they reflect the things we have just talked about:

- Over-serving the top 20% of your clients, using a written services timeline;

- Leveraging this top 20% for personal introductions to top prospects;

- Spending time on pre-call strategy to make the most effective use of your competitive advantage;

- Meeting with new prospects and winning; and

- Cross-selling and rounding out your clients to increase your revenue per client.

Typically, many advisors spend only about 20% of their time directly involved in these five activities and struggle with making the transition. I don't know if it's a lack of motivation or just fear. Here's what got me going.

I was in Houston doing a meeting on a Monday morning. One of the advisors walked in a little late that morning. As I checked to see if he was OK, he told me he'd been out late the night before. As I inquired why, he told me how he'd been on a long road trip, taking his daughter off to college, about a 10 hour drive. He went on to tell me about pulling the U-haul trailer with some of her furniture and luggage, and how he had to haul it up 3 flights of stairs mostly by himself, and then endured the long drive back to Houston. When his story was over, I looked him square in the eyes and said, at least the good news is that its all paid for isn't it. With a frown he looked at me and said "no." At that point, I knew he was paying for this out of his own pocket, stressing the monthly cash flow.

Here's the irony. This man is a professional. He advises others to take care of this kind of a problem in advance, and yet he didn't follow his own advice.

Being the father of 4 daughters, that was like sending up a warning flare telling me to get myself on the fast-track. So I did, and so can you.

What's the key to making this kind of a business transition? Number One on your list is a good reason. My reason was simple. I didn't want to be struggling with finances in the future when I had the ability to do something about it now.

Many of us, especially earlier in life, live hand to mouth, salting away the little bit we can into retirement and education. As our income goes up, so does our lifestyle and the savings rate remains the same, even for many advisors. With this Million Dollar Producer formula, you can take control of your "now and future" by following the four steps we are outlining. You can double your income in 3 years, and, with this formula, you can do it and have a balanced life.

For Wholesalers:
Trophy Case or Fruit Stand

Your proactive services platform is just as important if you are a wholesaler. If you are a wholesaler, what matters most to advisors is what you do that your competition doesn't. Your challenge is to get your advisors to see how they are being underserved by the incumbent wholesaler.

Most wholesalers lean on products, relationships, returns, and reactive service. They don't sell their proactive services, in fact many have never thought of it from this perspective. These potential competitive advantages remain hidden secrets that are not identified and articulated.

When I've been with groups of 20, 40, or 60 wholesalers and have asked them what makes them different and better, they have recited such things as their financials, relationships with advisors, and technology—the very things that actually make them the same.

I repeat: Your job as a wholesaler is to proactively control the experiences of your advisors and make their future more predictable. Your proactive services and your written services timeline make this possible. That's where you will find the underlying concrete things you do that differentiate you, and make advisors *want* to do business with you.

If you're a wholesaler, you're like a catcher in baseball. You are trying to attract the best pitches to home plate and win the game. On the mound is a star producer like Roger Clemmons, the five-time Cy Young Award winner. You signal Roger for the throws you want, but he shrugs you off. On the mound, he has a trophy case of his best accounts, and a fruit stand of hairy coconuts, sour lemons, mushy tomatoes, and fragile watermelons.

The challenge for you is to get the advisor to reach into his trophy case and throw you his best accounts. Why won't the advisor do this for you? As we've just discussed, it's because you don't truly differentiate why you are better. What you say makes you better—competitive returns, accessibility, and good products—only makes you the same as everyone else. You need to leverage your true competitive advantage in order to get into the trophy case. You need to get the advisor to see how he is being underserved by the incumbent whole-saler and go after his trophy accounts. Your price and product differences are too marginal for you to use to do that.

If you are like some wholesalers, you have a high closing ratio. Your problem is that you need more and better flow from advisors, better accounts to write. If returns and products won't get you that, what will? Not your reactive service. Nearly all wholesalers are good at putting out fires and fixing problems. So what will? Your *proactive* services, the things you do without being asked that make life better for the Advisor. That's where your most powerful differentiation and your competitive advantage lie.

Your CEO does not want to hear that you got the deal because you were cheaper. He wants to hear that you sold the value proposition, that you won the business because you were better. The CEO's focus is on profitable growth, not merely on a higher volume of low-margin business.

As a wholesaler, your job for an advisor is the same as the advisor's job for a client. It is to proactively control the experience of your advisor to make his or her future more predictable—and to bring those trophy accounts safely past home plate before the incumbent wholesaler standing in the batter's box can swat them away.

In a larger sense, however, competition never really goes away. As the late columnist Ann Landers once said, "Anyone who believes that the competitive spirit in America is dead has never been in a supermarket when the cashier opens another checkout line."

In our changing competitive landscape, the strategy of driving a "wedge" between your prospects and their incumbent service providers will remain more important than ever.

Appendix

"The Wedge" is a tool. Like any other tool, you have to practice with it.

In this appendix, we have provided you with several tools to help you. There are scripting tools for the rehearsal, Convincer Strategy, and best Deal Close.

Write your own scripts and practice them on your sales associates before using them with prospects. For additional information on developing and scripting Wedges or for other information regarding The Wedge, contact us at www.thewedge.net/FA.

Components of
The Prospect Interview

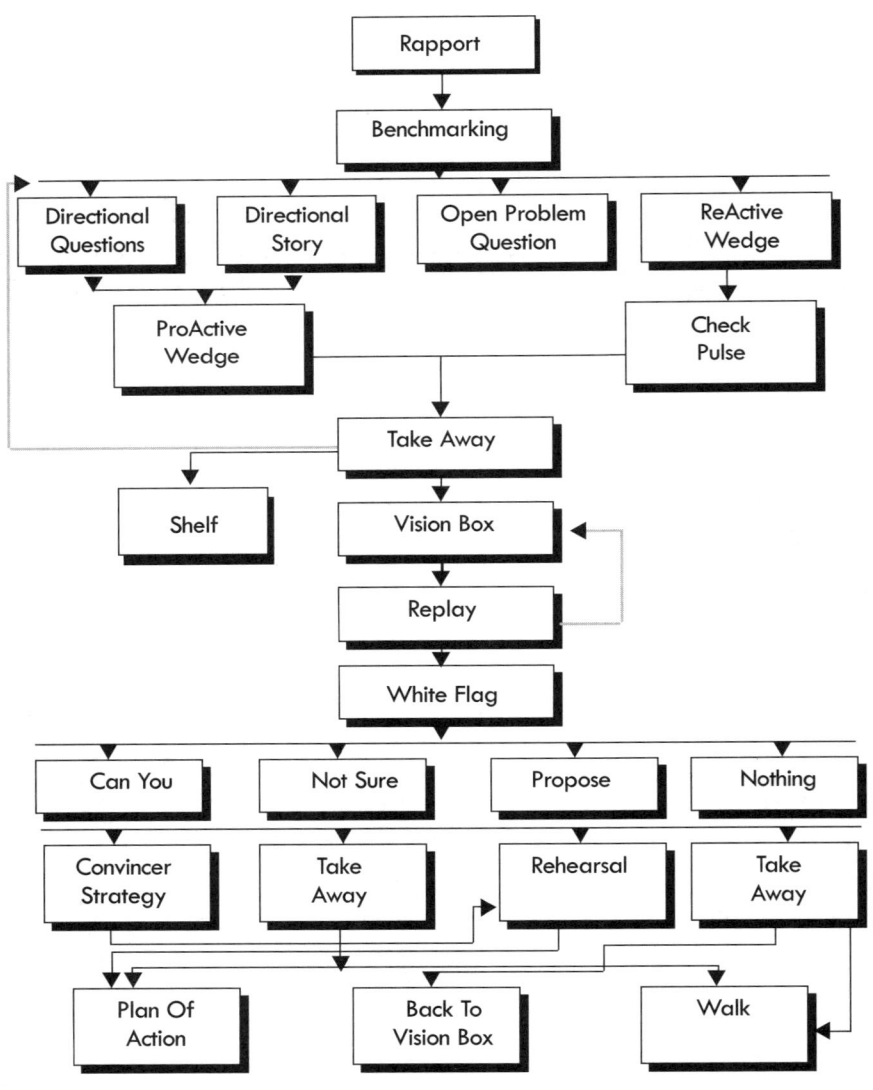

Rehearsal Script

Script out your **Rehearsal** - play off of...

S: Suppose for a moment that it's three weeks from now and you're looking at my proposal. It has all the elements you said you wanted. Can you imagine that?

P: OK, I can imagine that

S: As you look at the proposal you say to yourself, I think we've found a new Advisor. But that creates a new dilemma and I'm wondering, can we deal with that?

P: What is that?

S: The problem is that when you decide I'm your new guy, how are you going to tell the other guy that it's over?

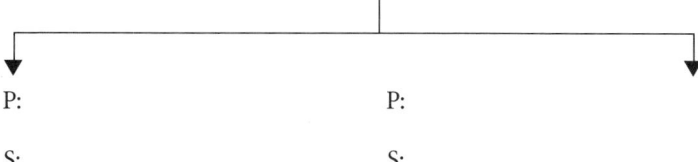

P: P:

S: S:

Convincer Strategy

Script out your **Convincer Strategy** - play off of...

P: Can you do that?

S: Sure, we can do that, but you expect me to say that don't you? Because you still see me as a salesperson, right?

P: Yes, I do.

S: So, how would you know that what I'm telling you is true...that we can do that? Do have to see letters of reference or an action plan? Do you have to talk to some people and let them tell you we can do it? Or, do you rely on your gut feeling to say, Yes, he's telling me the truth or no, he's lying to me. How would you know that what I'm telling you is true, that we really can do this?

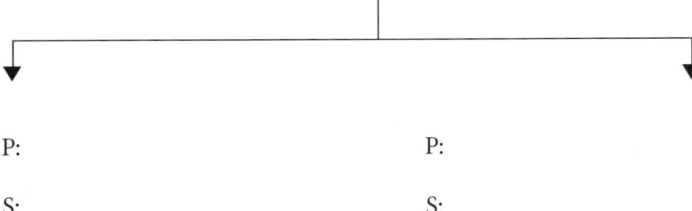

P: P:

S: S:

What's your Super Power?

- ▶ the power to **identify a need**
- ▶ the power to **formulate a strategy**
- ▶ the power to **sincerely benefit clients**
- ▶ the power to **increase your marketing potential**

Celebrating More Than
110 YEARS
NU CO

BONUS OFFER!

2 Is Better Than 1

Receive a FREE copy of *But What If I Live? The American Retirement Crisis®* when you buy **HOW TO PLAN for Baby Boomers Power Kit + HOW TO PLAN for College Power Kit Bundle of 2.** (512619K)

RETURN POLICY
100% Satisfaction Guaranteed

National Underwriter is confident you'll be pleased with our powerful resources. Your total satisfaction is guaranteed 100% of the time. If your expectations are not met or a product is damaged in shipping, contact us within 30 days from the invoice date for immediate resolution. Your purchase is refundable in the form of your original payment. Special rules apply for certain items:
1) CE Exams, Electronic Products, CD-ROMs, and Shipping & Handling are not refundable.
2) Subscriptions to newspapers, periodicals and loose-leaf services may be cancelled within 30 days from delivery of a first installment. Loose-Leaf services must be returned for a full refund.

....

SHIPPING & HANDLING

Order		Total	S&H
$0	to	$39.99	$7.95
$40.00	to	$79.99	$9.95
$80.00	to	$124.99	$12.95
$125.00	to	$199.99	$16.95
$200.00	to	$249.99	$19.95

....

Add shipping and handling charges to all orders as indicated. If your order exceeds total amount listed in chart, or for overseas rates, call 1-800-543-0874. **Any order of 10 or more items or $250 and over will be billed for shipping by actual weight, plus a handling fee.** Any discounts do not apply to Shipping & Handling.

QTY	ITEM DESCRIPTION	PRODUCT #	LIST PRICE	PROMO PRICE	TOTAL PRICE
	But What If I Live? Book	1890000	$21.95	$19.95	
	HOW TO PLAN for Baby Boomers Book	5120002	$38.10	$34.95	
	HOW TO PLAN for College Book	6190000	$38.10	$34.95	
	Garrett's Guide to Financial Planning Book & CD	2750002K	$52.27	$47.95	
	HOW TO PLAN for Baby Boomers Power Kit	5120002K	$81.70	$74.95	
	HOW TO PLAN for College Power Kit	6190000K	$81.70	$74.95	
	HOW TO PLAN Power Bundle (**Bonus Offer!**)	512619K	$163.40	$149.90	
	The Wedge for Financial Advisors	4700000	$38.10	$34.95	

Sales Tax: Residents of CA, CO, CT, DC, FL, GA, IL, KS, KY, MA, MI, NJ, NY, OH, PA, TX and WA must add appropriate sales tax

SUBTOTAL $ _____

Shipping & Handling (see chart) $ _____

ORDER TOTAL $ _____

Promo Code: GCARD
Offer Ends 12/30/08.

HOW TO PLAN Power Bundle
Offer Ends 12/30/08.

Discounts are based on a minimum purchase of the same title/product number. If you do not meet the minimum quantity to qualify for the printed discount, you will be invoiced the retail price.

☐ Invoice Me   ☐ Call Me

Company _____

Name _____   Title _____

Phone ( ) _____   E-mail _____

Address _____   Fax ( ) _____

City _____   State _____   Zip _____